TO

HUMPHREY

as always

and

to

All we love in Africa

'If your face is ugly, learn to sing.'
'Ukaipa nkhope, dziwa nyimbo.'

NYANJA PROVERB

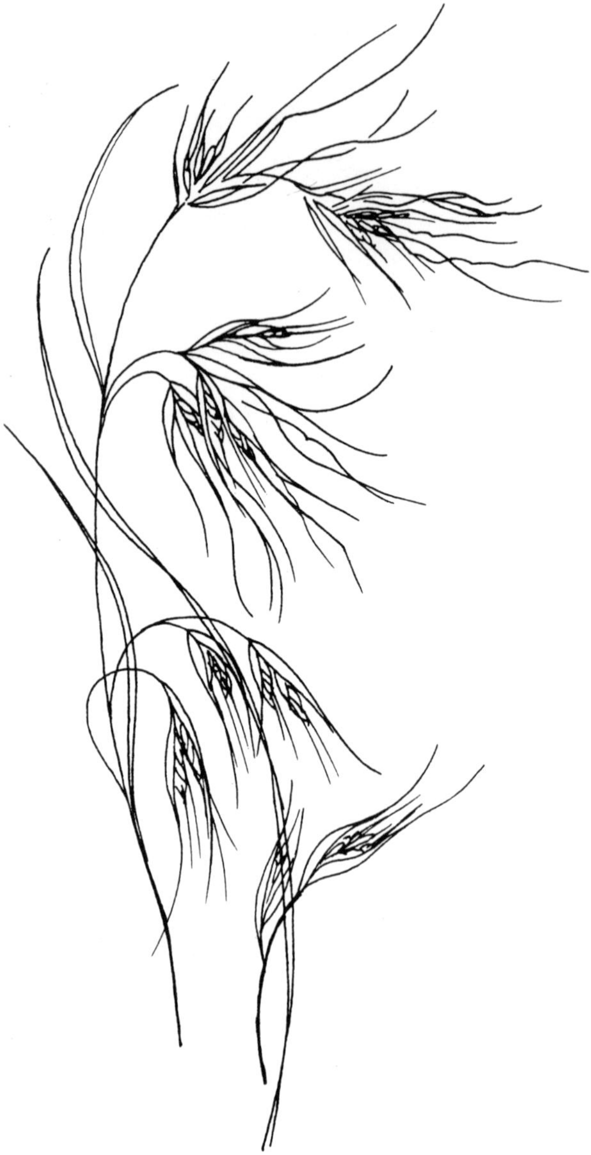

CONTENTS

THE SINGING CHAMELEON

GREY as the ancient rocks around him, Nadzikambe, the Chameleon, sat motionless, listening to the music of the stream. He was by nature a poet, and the sound of falling water always made him feel very poetical, especially if the sun were shining and the birds were gay and full of song. He listened for some time, then started to compose a poem that would do justice to the scene:

Birds singing
where the waters leap.
In the ripples,
silver fishes sleep.

Did they sleep in the ripples, he wondered? He must remember to ask the next fish he saw—not that it would make any difference to his poem if they didn't, but he would like to know. The Kingfisher probably could tell him, but Nadzikambe had no intention of asking him, conceited creature that he was. Admittedly, he was so beautiful that perhaps he had a right to be conceited. The Chameleon thought this over and decided, no. It was Mlungu, the Great Spirit, who had made the Kingfisher beautiful, just as Mlungu had made Chameleons plain, and neither the one nor the other deserved any credit or blame. After all, Nadzikambe reflected, beauty wasn't everything. Take the Lark, for instance, who was singing so gaily overhead—quite a plain and colourless bird, really, but you forgot that when listening to his lovely limpid notes.

Like a falling jewel, the Kingfisher dived into the stream, and the Lark stopped singing and came to rest beside the Chameleon.

'Wonderful to be so beautiful and to be able to dive like that,' said the Lark, his voice full of admiration.

'Yes,' agreed the Chameleon, 'but far more wonderful to be able to sing as you do.'

The Lark looked pleased. 'It's a pity you don't sing,' he said rather patronizingly. 'You ought to learn to do something, you know. Nobody should be useless. And my grandmother always used to say, "If your face is ugly, learn to sing." '

Nadzikambe, the Chameleon, swivelled one gloomy eye towards the Lark, and the corners of his mouth took on a dismal droop.

'All right,' he grumbled. 'I know I'm ugly and useless, but there's no need to rub it in. At least I can make myself almost invisible.'

'Oh, dear! I didn't mean . . . I'm sorry . . . you mustn't think . . . er . . . yes, of course. . . .' The Lark gabbled a confusion of apologies, then hurriedly said he must be going and soared into the air.

Nadzikambe watched him until he was no more than a speck of darkness in the blue vault of the sky. Then, from the distant height, he heard the limpid voice break into song once more. The Chameleon sighed. Oh, to be able to sing like that!

'If your face is ugly, learn to sing.' So the Lark's grandmother had said that, had she? Nadzikambe considered the little bird's advice. Learn to sing? Well, why not? Why shouldn't he learn to sing? Even if he could not hope to have a voice like the Lark's, he might still sing well enough to give pleasure and amusement to others as well as to himself. And he could sing his own poems . . . he might even learn to play the *bangwe* . . . and if he played well enough and sang well enough, perhaps nobody would taunt him any more with being slow and ugly and useless. It certainly was an idea—in fact, it was a splendid idea!

In a rush of enthusiasm Nadzikambe decided he would make himself a *bangwe* at once. All he'd need was a suitable piece of palm wood, a gourd and seven strings. Nothing difficult about that—he knew where to find them, and there was no point in wasting time. At top speed he set off for the place where the palm trees grew.

I am Nadzikambe,
the Chameleon who sings.
If your face is ugly,
it is wise to learn to sing.

I am Nadzikambe!
My colour's what I will:
Green as the tree fern,
Crimson as the aloe,
Golden as the sunset,
Purple as the hill.

There was no doubt that the Chameleon's voice was improving. True, it was not very musical, but it had a certain charm, and by this time he could play the *bangwe* as well as anyone. The fishes in the pool said that they enjoyed his singing very much, and even the Kingfisher had complimented him on one occasion. The Lark had not been seen for some time, but Nadzikambe was hoping that he would return one day, for it was the Lark's opinion that he really valued.

I am Nadzikambe!
I have learnt to sing.
I have learnt to play the bangwe . . .

Nadzikambe paused. *Ping-ping-ping*, he strummed, while he tried to think of a last line to his song. But his

mind had gone blank, and anyway he thought it was a bad verse, so he was quite pleased when he saw Katumbu, the Otter, emerge from the river and clamber on to the rock beside him. He liked Katumbu, who was always kind and friendly, and when he saw the worried frown on the Otter's face, he wondered anxiously what could be the matter.

'Whatever has happened?' the Chameleon asked. 'You do look upset!'

'It's terrible! Terrible!' said the Otter, shaking the water from his sable coat. 'That such a thing should happen in our district! And what can we do?'

'What are you talking about?' Nadzikambe was completely bewildered by these remarks.

'Surely you have heard? Don't you know about the monster that has come, from goodness only knows where, who is ravaging the countryside? It eats whole sheep and goats and everyone goes in terror of their lives.'

'What sort of monster? What does it look like?'

'Nobody knows. Nobody has seen it.'

'Can no one kill or capture it?'

'The Chief is offering great rewards to anyone who can rid us of the brute.'

Nadzikambe said nothing. Slowly he blinked, first one eye and then the other. What a fine thing it would be, he was thinking, if he were big and strong and brave and could capture the monster and win the great rewards. But what could one small Chameleon do? Nothing, save count himself lucky that he was neither a sheep nor a goat and so unattractive that even a hungry monster would not be likely to want to eat him. That, he supposed, was a comforting thought.

'The Chief is calling a meeting to which everyone is bidden,' Katumbu was saying, 'but I shouldn't think there is much point in your going. It is to be held tomorrow night, and I doubt if you could get there in time.'

'I'd like to go,' the Chameleon said quickly. A meeting would almost certainly mean an opportunity to play and sing and, anyway, he didn't want to miss anything exciting. 'Couldn't you take me with you?' he asked the Otter.

'How do you mean? Sitting on my head while I swim down the river?' Katumbu considered the idea for a moment, then: 'Yes,' he said. 'Why not? It might be a little risky for you, though.'

'Who minds taking risks?' demanded Nadzikambe in a richly swaggering tone. 'Not me!'

'Very well. Let's have luncheon right away and a short rest. Then we'll set off.'

'That suits me,' said the Chameleon and, while Katumbu slid back into the stream and got himself a couple of fresh young crabs, Nadzikambe, with his sticky tongue, picked off three gnats and five annoying but exceptionally delicious flies, gobbled them up and, with a comfortable feeling of repletion, settled down to sleep.

Some two hours later he and Katumbu woke up and, feeling greatly refreshed, they started out on their journey. And very peculiar they looked with Nadzikambe, his precious *bangwe* clutched beneath one foreleg, balancing with grim determination on the flat raft of the Otter's head!

The voyage, on the whole, was uneventful, for Katumbu knew the river well, and wherever there were dangerous rapids to negotiate he made a detour overland. At sunset they stopped for supper, and when they had eaten, Nadzikambe took his *bangwe* and began to sing a new song:

I had no canoe,
I had no raft,
I could not swim
down the river.

I had a friend,
Katumbu, the Otter.
He is my canoe,
he is my raft,
with him I am swimming
down the river.

Katumbu laughed. 'That's a fine song,' he said. 'And you sing and play it very well!'

'Hear, hear!' croaked a Bullfrog, who had just hopped on to the bank. 'Sing it again!'

'No, not now. We've a long way to go and we can't afford to waste time. We really must go "swimming down the river"!' The Otter attempted to sing the line, and the Chameleon and the Bullfrog joined in. So did a number of other animals, until there was quite a chorus singing round the pool: 'Let's go swimming down the river,' and when the Otter and the Chameleon set off once more, they were escorted for a short distance by a happy, laughing throng.

They travelled until the moon went down, slept until dawn, had breakfast and continued their journey. Midday found them near the place where the river plunged a hundred feet or more into a wild gorge. Above the fall, the water flowed calmly enough, though the current was strong, and the river was spanned by a swinging bridge of rope. Here Katumbu decided to call a halt, for it was no great distance from the village of Chief Ngamo, where the meeting was to be held and, leaving the Chameleon safely hidden in a clump of lilies, he went off in search of luncheon.

The scent of the lilies attracted flies, so it was an ideal spot for Nadzikambe and, in no time at all, he had eaten more than enough. He then fell asleep and soon he was dreaming that he was playing his *bangwe* and singing to a large circle of animals: Kalulu, the Rabbit; Kamba, the Tortoise; Changa, the Lemur; they were all there and it was all very delightful. But suddenly they turned into sheep and goats and, instead of laughing and applauding, they began to hiss and one goat gave a high-pitched screech. . . .

Nadzikambe woke up and shook himself. What a nice dream it had been to start with, he thought, but really that screech had seemed too real! Oh, well, indigestion always gave him nightmares and he knew he'd done himself too well on those flies! He stretched and began to move slowly on to one of the long green lily-buds, turned to just the same shade of green, and looked around.

It was a beautiful spot and the distant thunder of the fall came like music to his ears. Not far from him a tree—a pale cloud of sunlit blossom—cast its gentle shade over a large rock. The tree, alone, Nadzikambe felt, deserved a poem, and he took his *bangwe* from beneath his foreleg, struck a few chords, and began to sing:

The sun
lights
the blossom
of the
Wild Plum.
Soon,

so soon,
the blossoms
fall.

'Charming! Charming! Who is singing?' There was a slight hissing note in the thick voice, and Nadzikambe looked around to see who had spoken. At first there seemed to be no one, then the Chameleon noticed that the rock beneath the Plum Tree had changed its shape and that it appeared to be moving. Fascinated, he watched it uncoil itself and rear its head and he realized with a shock that the rock was not a rock at all, but quite the biggest Python imaginable.

'How I love music!' The creature gave a sigh. 'It is such a help to one's digestion and, really, some of these old sheep and goats do give one a pain!'

The Chameleon laughed and started to play again. Poor old Python, he thought. A nice creature, fond of music. So he suffered from indigestion, too, did he? Well, if music was a help, of course he'd go on singing. Nadzikambe wondered what he should sing to soothe the pain the sheep and goats had caused . . . sheep and goats? . . . SHEEP AND GOATS!!! But that was what the monster ate! Oh, my! Could it be? Was this? Yes, of course, it must be the monster!

In his alarm and excitement the Chameleon nearly fell off the lily-bud. What was he to do? What could he do? If only he could capture the creature! But how? How? If only Katumbu would come back. . . .

'Go on singing, whoever you are. I want music. Music fascinates me. Music enchants me.' The Python's

head began to sway from side to side in time to an imaginary rhythm. 'Go on! Sing!'

What, oh, what to do? The Chameleon swivelled his eyes round and round in an effort to think of a plan. If the monster really did love music—and, now he came to think of it, he had heard that snakes could be charmed by music—could he not lure this one into a trap of some sort? Yes, but what trap? Traps had to be set—they didn't just happen!

'Sing!' The Python spoke impatiently. 'Sing, when I tell you to!'

Should he obey? Yes, Nadzikambe decided. Better humour the monster, at least until Katumbu had returned. Meanwhile, might it not be wise to move on to the bridge? He'd be safer there and, once across the river, perhaps he could get help from the village? He hurried down the lily-stem and started to play again. '*Olé, olé!*' he sang.

Olé!
Unseen,
Invisible,
  I am
  the Spirit of Music.
In the blowing wind
  am I,
In the falling rain
  am I,
In the water's roar
  am I,
Invisible,

Unseen.
I am
the Spirit of Music.

'Beautiful!' sighed the Python, swaying a little and gliding forward. 'How I wish that I could see you!'

'Unseen, invisible am I,' sang Nadzikambe, hoping it was true. He reached the bridge and, still singing, climbed on to the rope. By now the Python was swaying steadily and a far-away look had come into its little eyes. As if in a trance, it glided towards the sound of the music.

It is following me, thought Nadzikambe. I've bewitched the monster and it is following me. If I keep on playing, if I keep on singing, perhaps it will come all the way to the village? If only I knew how far it is to the village! If only Katumbu would come back!

Singing loudly and balancing as best he could, Nadzikambe slowly made his way along the rope. The Python slithered after him, but no sooner had its heavy body touched the rope, than the whole bridge began to rock and shake and, next moment, a sudden lurch sent the Chameleon hurtling into the river below.

'Help!' he yelled. 'Help!' as he sank into the cool green waters, down, down and down. I'm lost, he thought, I shall drown. Oh, if only I could swim! Then a big claw grabbed him and he felt himself borne upwards and, choking and spluttering, but still clasping his precious *bangwe*, he was carried swiftly to the bank. Katumbu, the Otter, had come back in the nick of time.

Night had fallen. In the *bwalo* at Ngamo's village a bright fire blazed, illuminating the anxious faces of the people as they listened to their Chief. The tale of the monster's ravages had been told, a sorry tale of sheep and goats that vanished in broad daylight, of frightened pigs, of hens too scared to lay their eggs.

'Have our trappers lost their cunning?' demanded Ngamo. 'Have our hunters lost their skill? Can no one rid us. . . .' He broke off suddenly and looked up, listening intently. Someone was singing, singing like a Lark. A moment later, a small bird flew down and hopped up to the Chief.

'News, Mfumu!' he cried. 'I bring great news! The monster is captured and we are saved. Nadzikambe, the Chameleon, and his friend, Katumbu, have saved us all!'

'Nadzikambe?' asked the Chief, his eyes wide with amazement, and an incredulous murmur rose from the crowd. 'How could Nadzikambe . . . how is this possible?'

As briefly as he could, the Lark told his story. He told how the Chameleon had found the monster, the great Python that could be bewitched by music. He told of Nadzikambe's playing and his songs; of the fall into the river and Katumbu's rescue. He told of the plan that the friends had then made; how the Chameleon, perching on the Otter's head, had been carried across the river; how he had sung and sung, while the enchanted snake, heedless of all else but the music, had followed and been lured towards the falling water. The current had swept the monster away and it had been caught, some distance below the falls, in the fishermen's nets. A great prize for the fishermen!

'Is this true?' asked Ngamo. 'With whose eyes did you see this happen?'

'With my own eyes, Mfumu,' replied the Lark. 'I was flying near the river and I saw it all.'

'And where are Nadzikambe and Katumbu now?'

'On their way here.'

'Then we will go and meet them.' Ngamo clapped his hands and the people rose excitedly to their feet. The drummers ran to their drums, the musicians to their gourds. Singing and dancing, the whole village streamed out to greet the heroes.

Later that night, amidst great rejoicing, a feast was held. Honours and riches were heaped on Nadzikambe and Katumbu and, with full ceremonial, they were granted Insect and Fishing Rights over a wide stretch of the river. They sat, one each side of Chief Ngamo, and again and again were asked to tell the story of the afternoon's adventure.

'You tell a story well,' said the Chief to Nadzikambe. 'You shall be my Teller of Tales, my Chief Minstrel and the Singer of Songs. Will you not sing to us now?'

'Yes! Yes!' cried everyone. 'Sing to us, Nadzikambe! Give us a song!'

The Chameleon rose and bowed. Slowly his eyes travelled round the firelit circle. It was all too good to be true! Here was he, no longer despised by everyone but a popular hero and, now, he was actually being asked to sing! He picked up his *bangwe*, cleared his throat and took a deep breath:

I am Nadzikambe,
the Chameleon who sings.

'Delightful,' murmured the Lark, and the Chameleon smiled happily.

If your face is ugly,
it is wise to learn to sing.

'How true!' said someone.

'How wise my grandmother was,' murmured the Lark.

'Grandmothers are wise,' said the Chief.

'Yes, indeed,' agreed the Chameleon and went on with his song.

THE GOAT AND THE EAGLE

'MAA! Maa!' The little white Goat stood bleating wistfully as he looked around the dusty village. He had come from a place in the high hills—brought by his owner as a formal present to the Chief—and now he felt lonely, lost and friendless and he longed to be back amongst the mountains that he loved. He gave a little tug at the lead that tethered him to a tree. If only he could get free, he decided, he'd go skipping back to the soft green grass, the singing streams, the old grey rocky hills that had been his cradle and his father's father's home.

Nadzikambe, the Chameleon, heard the bleating and swivelled an eye towards the sound. He saw the little white Goat below, thought he looked unhappy, so moved down the tree-trunk in order to get closer. Maybe he needed a friend?

'Good morning,' said Nadzikambe. 'You don't sound very cheerful! Can I help you at all?'

The little Goat looked at the Chameleon. 'I want to go home,' he replied, simply.

'And where is home?' Nadzikambe asked.

'High up in those mountains.' He raised his eyes and pointed to a distant range of magical blue peaks. 'We have lived there ever since my ancestor, Mbuzi, found the cave and wore his Eagle feathers.'

'Ah! That was your ancestor, was it?' Nadzikambe was all interest. 'I scarcely know the story and have always wished to hear it. If you will tell it to me, perhaps I could . . . er . . . well now, you don't want that tiresome lead round your neck when you are telling a story, do you?'

'Oh!' breathed the little Goat. 'Would you really unfasten it for me?' He looked again at the far-off hills, his bright eyes full of hope. 'If only you would do that, I will gladly tell you the tale.'

Mbuzi was as handsome a young Goat as anyone could wish to see. His coat was creamy-white and gleamed in the sunshine like a pearl. A little silky beard adorned his chin. He carried his head proudly, for the time had come for him to take a wife and he knew that Msoti, the little white Goat of his choice, would come to him as soon as he could offer her a home.

And so, a home was what he had to find: a fine home that would be a shelter from the wind and rain, from storm and fire, from fierce and dangerous neighbours, and from all the perils that can beset a Goat. That such a place existed he felt sure, for often he had dreamt of such a cave. Again and again, in his sleep, he had seen a pile of ancient rocks spilling upon an apron of grass and, close at hand, a spring of crystal water that bubbled to the surface and went tiptoeing away to form a little mountain stream. That was the place that he now hoped to find: that was the spot for which he was searching.

On and on he wandered, moving higher and higher into the hills. He passed through the woodlands where his Kudu cousins lived; he passed through the emerald valleys where his Zebra cousins grazed; in time he came to the grassy uplands, where the turf was short and springy and a myriad irises danced in the breeze, like a host of brilliant butterflies.

Mbuzi stood quite still for some minutes, breathing in the mountain air and looking all around. Away on his right, a little stream seemed to beckon . . . perhaps it would lead him to the spring? He decided to follow it.

It did. With a bleat of delight, the white Goat recognized the boulders, sprang on to the apron of grass, ran and found the entrance to the cave. This was it! This was the cave of his dream! So excited was he that Mbuzi never saw the skulking form that had been following him, oh, so stealthily, ever since he'd left the Zebras' valley.

As soon as the Goat had finished exploring the cave, which showed no signs of habitation, he made a ceremonial fire at the entrance, then went off to fetch a bundle of sweet grasses for an offering to the Spirits of his Ancestors who, in their wisdom, had led him to the place. It took rather longer to find them than he had expected, but what did time matter? It was a wonderful world, a wonderful day, and now he had a wonderful home!

When Mbuzi got back, it was to find that someone else had occupied his wonderful home. Fisi, the Hyaena, looking smug and self-satisfied, sat at the mouth of the cave, warming himself beside the ceremonial fire.

The Goat's heart sank. Of all people, Fisi was one of the least desirable to have around the place. And what was Fisi doing, sitting there as if he owned the cave? Mbuzi didn't like the look of things at all.

'Ah! A stranger in these parts, surely?' The Hyaena had an odious smirk. 'Welcome to my cave!'

'What do you mean, "your cave"? There were no signs of ownership when I found it,' the Goat protested quickly.

'I fear you can't have looked very carefully.' Fisi shook his head in a reproving manner. 'Though I'd have thought you must have seen my sign above the entrance?' He pointed to an amulet, made from a Hyaena's claw and hair, that now dangled from a stick stuck in a crevice of the rock.

'That was not there when I got here first. There was

nothing here, not even the ashes of a fire. I made the ceremonial fire, as you well know. The cave is mine!' Mbuzi's voice quivered with indignation.

'You made the fire?' queried Fisi. 'Poor fellow! How sad! You have imagined it all! I made this fire, myself. This is my ceremonial fire and the cave belongs to me.' The Hyaena smiled blandly and with the utmost assurance.

'That is a lie!'

'Well,' said the Hyaena, 'the only way to settle the matter is to speak a case. Mkango, the Lion, holds his Court tomorrow. Let us take our case to him.'

In angry silence, the Goat considered the suggestion. It was, he supposed, the only thing to do, though he had little faith in the Lion as a judge. But he had faith in his ancestors, and surely their spirits would not let him lose the cave now that he had found it?

The case was over. Mkango, the Lion, had given his verdict: since it was a question of the word of one complainant against the word of another, with no supporting evidence, the Hyaena and the Goat must share the cave. One would hunt by night, the other by day, and the one who first failed to bring home the meat would be the one to forfeit the cave. The Lion himself would come and live with them, to see that neither cheated and, of course, to share their dinners. Surely an admirable judgement? What could be fairer?

Or, thought Mbuzi, the Goat, what could be more unfair? It was all a plot, for the Lion knew quite well that Goats did not kill. Goats did not go hunting,

Goats only ate grass and herbs. How could he bring back a buck, or even a fowl or a goose? And not only once, but again and again, until he failed to do so and had to leave his new-found home.

What, he wondered miserably, was he to do? Abandon the cave? No, he couldn't bear to do that. Learn to make traps? Well, he could try, but could he hope to catch anything at the first attempt? No. And, anyway, he didn't want to catch anything.

All the time he had been thinking these thoughts, Mbuzi had been climbing higher and higher up the mountain and now, worn out with worry, he lay down on a rock and soon fell fast asleep.

Far above, poised almost motionless in the blue vault of the heavens, Mphambe, the Eagle, gazed at the earth below with eyes that noted every detail of the scene—a Bushbuck grazing in a grassy hollow; a school of Guinea-fowl searching at the edge of a thicket for grubs and insects for their morning meal; a Mongoose scurrying across a path; a white Goat lying on a rock. So still did the white goat seem that the Eagle thought it might, perhaps, be dead, and he decided to have a closer look. Mphambe dropped down and came to rest beside the sleeping figure.

With a start, the Goat woke up and grabbed hold of the Eagle's leg. He blinked and looked up at the great bird. 'Why!' cried Mbuzi in amazement, 'I've caught you!'

'What do you mean?' said the Eagle, equally surprised. 'I just thought you might be dead and came to have a look. What do you mean, you've caught me? *You* don't catch your fellow creatures!'

'Well, I never have before,' the Goat admitted, 'but now I've got to, or I shall lose my home.'

'What are you talking about?' The Eagle did not know what to make of the Goat's extraordinary behaviour. 'Would you mind explaining? And let go my leg, there's a good fellow!'

'I can't do that. I dare not let you go,' said Mbuzi, and he began to explain the predicament in which he had been placed. The Eagle listened with attention and rising indignation, as he learned of the Hyaena's mean plot.

'What a scoundrel!' Mphambe exclaimed. 'But we'll defeat him. I will do your killing for you, though it will need more than that to drive him altogether away. I think it will need cunning and, perhaps, a little magic. Now, take these three feathers'—the Eagle took three feathers from his underwing—'and when you go out hunting, place one in the cleft of each hoof, using both your hind legs and your left fore hoof. Then, when you see your quarry, stand behind it and point your feathered foreleg at it. Leave the rest to me.'

'How can I thank you enough?' asked the Goat.

'There is no need to thank me,' said the Eagle with a smile. 'Remember that you caught me and let me go!'

'I can't understand it!' Fisi, the Hyaena, was puzzled and very disappointed that his plot had so far failed.

'D'you mean to say that Goat brings back a buck or something every day? It's incredible!' Mkango, the Lion, was equally mystified. 'How does he do it? He has never killed anything before. Perhaps he uses traps?'

'Perhaps. But I never see him making a trap.' The Hyaena scratched his head and frowned. 'All he ever takes with him is three feathers. Now, what good could they be?'

'Feathers, eh?' The Lion gnawed his claws for a moment, then: 'They wouldn't be magic feathers, by any chance?' he asked, a little nervously.

'Magic feathers? Oh, my! I never thought of that!'

'Well, you'd better start thinking about it now,' said the Lion, 'because that's probably what they are.' The two animals looked at each other with very glum expressions. They didn't like the idea of magic feathers at all, especially if they had fatal properties!

'We'd better find out more about them,' growled the Hyaena. 'We must watch that Goat. I'll follow him tomorrow. We must know what happens.'

So, next morning, when Mbuzi set out for his day's hunting, Fisi, the Hyaena, feigned sleep until he'd left the cave. Then he got up and, with the utmost caution, he trailed the Goat. That evening he told the Lion what he had seen.

'They are magic feathers, all right,' Fisi reported. 'I followed him until he came upon a herd of Reedbuck. Then, what d'you think he did? Stuck the feathers in his hooves, got behind a buck and pointed one feathered foreleg in its direction!'

'What then?' asked the Lion, with breathless interest.

'Mind you,' the Hyaena continued, 'I couldn't see too well from where I was hiding, but it seemed as if some object dropped from the skies and, next minute, there was the buck lying dead. I didn't like it, I can tell you!'

'I don't like it either,' said the Lion. 'I've been asking questions since I saw you last, and everyone tells the same story. The Goat puts feathers in his hooves, stands behind his quarry and points one feather at it. Then *whoosh!* Something falls from the skies and the victim lies dead.' The Lion gave a shudder. 'I don't like it at all. Supposing the Goat gets behind you and points his feather? How'll you like that?'

Fisi's jaw dropped in dismay. 'You don't think he'd do that?' he quavered.

'Why shouldn't he?' Mkango almost sounded pleased at the idea.

'Well, if it comes to that, why shouldn't he get behind you? How would you like that?'

'But he's got no reason. . . .' The Lion almost squeaked in his alarm. 'Why should Mbuzi point his feather at me? What have I done?'

'You gave the judgement, didn't you?'

'What's wrong with my judgement?' Mkango demanded. 'It was a very good judgement, very clever. And let me remind you,' he snarled, 'that you haven't caught anything yet tonight. You'd better be off, or it will be you who forfeits the cave!'

The Hyaena gave the Lion a very sour look, opened his mouth to say something, thought better of it and, growling darkly, stalked off without another word.

All the way to his usual hunting-ground, Fisi's mind brooded over the magic feathers and the idea that the Goat might one day come behind and point his feather at him. Every now and then, he glanced nervously over his shoulder to make sure he was not being followed.

If a pebble rolled, his heart missed a beat. At the snapping of a twig he leapt like a startled Duiker. At the hooting of an Owl he yelped aloud and started to run. . . .

He reached the hunting-ground only to find it deserted. There seemed to be no sign of any living creature. Perhaps, thought Fisi, all the birds and beasts had gone away, scared by the Goat and his hateful magic feathers? If that were so, then where was he to find a dinner? And if he failed to do so, as the Lion had said, it would be he who would forfeit the cave. Well, he asked himself, did that matter so much? Certainly, it was an ideal cave, but he had really only occupied it out of spite. He could find another, miles and miles away, in another part of the country, where there were no Goats with magic feathers or bolts that fell from heaven if anybody stood behind you. Far, far better to go away, Fisi decided. After all, it would be no disgrace to return with empty paws, for Mbuzi was to blame. Obviously, the Goat had scared the game away and, if there was no game about, how could anyone catch anything? Of course, there was nothing left to catch. Who in the world would be so foolish as to remain anywhere near that Goat? Certainly not himself. Oh, dear, no! No cave was worth it!

His mind made up, the Hyaena retraced his steps and told the Lion of his decision.

'Well,' snorted Mkango, 'I can't say I blame you. In fact, I've decided to go away myself. I find I prefer the tawny plains to these green windy hills. And, no doubt, now there will be plenty of game down there.

The Goat may have done us a good turn after all—"He who has not one thing, has another", as the proverb says. Let the Goat have his cave, I say, and let us get away from him and his feathers just as quickly as we can.'

'And so,' said the little white Goat, as he finished his tale, 'the cave has belonged to us ever since and our family has lived peacefully and happily in the high hills.'

'Very interesting,' murmured the Chameleon. 'And what became of the Eagle feathers?'

'There are three feathers in our amulet,' replied the Goat, 'but I do not think they are the ones Mbuzi wore. Long ago those feathers must have crumbled into dust. And, of course, there was no need to use them once the Hyaena had gone away.'

'I suppose not.' The Chameleon smiled at the little Goat. 'The Chief has many Goats,' he said, with meaning. 'Far more than he can number, and what is one Goat more or less to him? These Goats were mostly born down here and may not know your story. I think I must tell it to them at once. *Olé, olé!*' he shouted. 'Call all the Goats, for I have a tale to tell them!'

The little white Goat cocked his head on one side and looked at the Chameleon, and Nadzikambe grinned, raised his eyes to the distant range of mountains, then, slowly and deliberately, he winked. The little Goat grinned back. Joyfully he kicked up his heels, murmured a word of thanks and ran off to mingle with the village Goats, as they came wandering up to hear the Chameleon's story.

Overhead, poised almost motionless in the morning sky, an Eagle hovered and surveyed the earth below. His sharp eyes took in every detail of the scene—three women pounding corn; a Crocodile sunning itself upon the river-bank; the Chief sitting with his village Elders; a crowd of Goats, black Goats, brown Goats, white Goats, clustered round a tree, listening, perhaps, to some fascinating story? A solitary white Goat skipping along the track that led up to the mountains. Nothing very interesting, the Eagle decided. Now, if only he could spot something worth eating—a Snake, for instance—he could drop upon it like a bolt from the blue and, in a moment, he would be swallowing a delicious meal! Surely, there must be something worth having down there? The Eagle flapped his great wings and soared upwards to command a wider view.

Perched on a branch of the tree, Nadzikambe, the Chameleon, beamed at his audience, cleared his throat and began his tale.

'Mbuzi was as handsome a young Goat as anyone could wish to see. His coat. . . .'

THE TORTOISE AND THE LION

Above the river-bed, a soft white veil of mist shrouded the ancient trees and muted every sound. Even the song of the stream seemed hushed and the ferns leaned closer to the water, as if to catch each ripple's secret message.

'The Sanjika are on the run!'

'The Sanjika went by as I flowed over the black rock.'

'As I entered the Turtles' pool. . . .'

'As I swirled down the rapids. . . .'

'Hundreds of shining silver fishes.'

'They should reach the spawning-grounds tonight.'

'The Sanjika are on the run!'

Chule, the Frog, hopped on to the bank and hurried off. He, too, had seen the fish go by and he had promised to get word to his friend, the Tortoise, as soon as he could; for Kamba, the Tortoise, had the right to fish from one particular rock, and Chule knew how eagerly he was awaiting news of the run.

He found the Tortoise busily mending a net. 'Come on!' he said. 'There's no time to lose. If you make straight for your rock, you'll be able to scoop up all the fish you need. The Sanjika are on the run!'

'Hurrah! What splendid news!' Kamba bustled about, collecting his gear, then made off for the river at top speed.

Through the blanketing mist he went, his heart high, his eyes bright with visions of the fish he hoped to catch. Sanjika galore . . . an ugly Barbel or two . . . perhaps a Mpasa? That would be a triumph! He'd give a party for all his friends, and any fish left over could be dried in the sun and stored for later use. Oh, there was nothing to equal the thrill of fishing! And on a morning such as this, it was indeed an adventure.

Kamba, the Tortoise, reached the river and climbed on to his rock. The thick mist hemmed him in, so that he seemed to be the only living creature in a world of white. He peered down at the water, swirling whitely through a narrow channel, grasped his net and gently lowered it in. With baited breath he waited for the jerk that would tell him that he'd got a fish. Ah! . . . no . . . no . . . aha!

there it was! Excitedly, and with some difficulty, he raised the net. In it lay three wriggling silver bodies, three beautiful Sanjika. Kamba gave a chortle of delight and laid them reverently on the bank behind him; then he returned to his pitch and lowered the net again. He had not long to wait. Thick and fast the fish came tumbling in and, as swiftly as he could, he tossed them on to the bank and returned for more. Never had there been such a morning's fishing!

Through the blanketing mist stalked Mkango, the Lion. He was feeling thirsty and was making his way to the river for a drink. He thought it was an eerie morning, a morning when anything could happen; the trees might turn into witches; the stones might come alive—one rock looked very like a Water Monitor shamming dead, and beyond it lay . . . what was that silvery mound? He halted, peered through the mist, crept slowly forward, sniffed inquiringly . . . fish? Undoubtedly, there was a smell of fish—fresh fish! Mkango's mouth began to water. It was hungry he now felt, not thirsty! He crept closer still, reached out a cautious paw and grabbed a fish. He popped it into his mouth, swallowed it whole and grabbed another and another. Then he retired into the bushes to wait and see what happened.

For some minutes, nothing did. The mist had thinned a little and Mkango was on the point of rising when he noticed something moving on the bank. Whatever was it? It looked like Kamba, the Tortoise . . . Kamba dragging a net . . . it was the Tortoise! Mkango nearly laughed aloud. This was too easy! He got up and sauntered across.

'Ah! You're in luck, I see. That's a fine haul you've got there. Mind if I help myself?' Mkango did not wait for an answer; he just ate three more fishes in quick succession.

Kamba said nothing, but his spirits sank. It wasn't that he grudged the Lion a fish or two, seeing he had caught so many, but would Mkango be content with one or two? It didn't look like it. And if he were to go on fishing, the Lion might easily take the lot while his back was turned. Or some other creature might come along and help himself. Now the mist was lifting, his privacy was gone. What a dilemma to be in! Kamba could have cried when he thought of all the fish he was not catching; even though the main run was over, there were surely still some stragglers and perhaps an eel to be had. Dare he go back to his rock? No, the Lion was still eating, and now here was Nyalugwe, the Leopard!

'Do I smell fish?' The Leopard stood, inhaling blissfully. M'm! How delicious! Oh, hallo, Mkango, are they yours?'

'No,' said Kamba, shortly. 'They're mine. I caught them.'

'You're lucky. A fine haul.'

'It *was*,' said Kamba, pointedly.

'Mind if I have one?' asked Nyalugwe, helping himself.

'You may have two,' replied Kamba generously, hoping he'd be satisfied and go.

'Thank you, Kamba. You are very kind.' The Leopard

selected his fish, said good morning and wandered happily away.

The Tortoise gave a sigh of relief and Mkango stopped eating and looked up in surprise. 'Can't be hungry!' was his comment, as he watched the Leopard disappear. A wistful look had come into his eyes. 'Those spots!' he murmured. 'So handsome, so beautiful. I wish that I had spots!'

'I gave him his spots,' said Kamba carelessly.

'You did?'

'Yes.' It was, in fact, an ancestor of Kamba's who, according to legend, had given the Leopard spots and made him beautiful, in return for some small kindness.

'Could you give me spots?' Mkango was all eagerness.

The Tortoise looked thoughtfully at the Lion. Only one fish was now left and he was feeling bitter. The Lion deserved to be taught a lesson for his greed.

'Yes,' Kamba spoke with some hesitation, 'I could.'

'Now? At once?'

'Well, there are certain things I need before I can begin.'

'What things?'

'The hide of an antelope, cut into strips.'

'I can get that easily enough,' said the Lion. 'Shall I fetch it right away?'

'Yes.' Kamba was beginning to feel happier. Fetching the antelope hide would keep the Lion occupied for quite a little time; meanwhile he would be able to go back to his fishing.

'I shan't be long,' Mkango called out, as he ran off.

'No need to hurry,' shouted the Tortoise. He was

already on his way back to the rock. The mist had vanished and the sun now lit the tumbling waters and bejewelled the dripping ferns. Once more the Tortoise could let down his net.

For some time nothing moved. Evidently the Sanjika had gone past, so all poor Kamba had to show for his morning's toil was one small fish. He knew he couldn't give a party on just one fish! If only that wretched Lion had not come along! Or had been content, like Nyalugwe, with a couple of fish. If only. . . . A sudden jerk nearly wrenched the net from Kamba's paws. He raised the net, hung on desperately and, with all the determination he possessed, slowly brought his fish to land. Kamba could scarcely believe his luck. It was a glorious Mpasa, fine and fat and shining, enough for any feast! The next thing was to hide it, somewhere where it would be safe from envious, greedy eyes. A near-by clump of fern looked promising enough. . . .

The Tortoise had only just concealed his treasure, when Mkango came bounding back, dragging the skin of an old antelope.

'Here we are,' he cried. 'Now what about these strips?'

Bother, thought Tortoise, he has been quick; but at least I've got the big Mpasa and that should be safe. Aloud he said: 'I'll show you what I want.' He picked up a sharp stone and started to rip the skin into narrow thongs. 'See? Like that. Then we must have a ceremonial fire.'

Leaving Mkango to deal with the antelope hide, Kamba busied himself collecting sticks and brushwood, which he piled in the centre of an open patch of ground. He then went back to the Lion and picked up one of the thongs.

'We must make these into bracelets,' he said. 'There are four winds from which your spots can blow,' Kamba went on, speaking in a kind of chant. 'These trees are the winds' four messengers.' He beckoned to the Lion and made him stand between a group of trees. Then he slipped a thong round Mkango's forepaw and tied the other end securely to the nearest tree. 'Here is a bracelet from the North Wind, and here, a bracelet from the South.' He slipped a second thong around the opposite hind paw and tied it to another tree. 'A bracelet from the East,' he chanted, 'a bracelet from the West.' When he had finished, there was the Lion, bound to the four trees, quite, quite helpless.

'This is wonderful,' sighed the Lion. 'How soon will the spots appear?'

'Have patience,' said the Tortoise and returned to his fire. With some difficulty he got it going. Then, taking some sticks and stones and grass and some wet mud from the river, he set to work to make a small, rough effigy of the Lion. This he covered with a piece of hide. Mkango watched, fascinated.

When it was done, Kamba turned and blew upon the fire four times, from the North, the South, the East and the West. Then he began to circle round the effigy, chanting as he went:

The Lion has no spots!
Can the four winds
give them to him?

Yes, the winds will fan the fire.

Can the fire
give them to him?

Yes, the fire will heat the brand.

Can the Tortoise
give them to him?
Can the Tortoise
give him spots?

As he said 'spots', Kamba seized a stick from the fire and pressed its glowing, red-hot end upon the skin of the effigy. There was a sizzling sound, a smell of burning fur and, when he raised the stick, there was a fine black spot!

Trembling with excitement, Mkango turned his head and tried to see if, by this magic, a spot had appeared upon his own skin, but no, it was as plain and tawny as it had always been.

'It hasn't worked!' There was a world of disappointment in the Lion's voice.

'Of course not. I was only testing the brand on the effigy. It works splendidly.' Kamba beamed at the Lion and selected another glowing stick. 'Now we can brand the spots on you,' he said. 'How many would you like? One for every fish you've eaten?'

'What?' Mkango gazed at the Tortoise with unbelief.

'Or would you rather have no spots and give me a fish, or perhaps a little bag of beans, for every spot you have not got? You see,' Kamba explained, 'I was planning a party and you have robbed me of the food intended for my guests.'

'But you can't mean . . .' Mkango began, hoarsely. Then he gave a roar of rage and strained frantically at his bonds, but they had been securely tied and he could not break free.

'A spot for every fish you've eaten, or a fish, or bag of beans, for every spot you have not got?' repeated Kamba. 'Make up your mind.'

Mkango glared at the Tortoise and did some rapid thinking. He'd no intention of being branded like a thief. Those were not at all the kind of spots he wanted. He supposed he'd have to agree to hand over the fish or beans, but what did that matter? He need not carry out his promise—there were no witnesses! Once free. . . .

'Not much choice, have you?' Nadzikambe, the Chameleon, had suddenly appeared from nowhere, as he so often did. 'You'd much better agree to give Kamba what he asks—he is being more than fair—and I will see that you honour your pledge.'

The Lion looked very crestfallen. So there was a witness after all, and he would have to carry out his bargain!

'On the day your luck is out, even the cold porridge will burn you,' quoted Nadzikambe. 'These old proverbs are so true!'

'Very well,' said the Lion. 'Set me free and I will go and fetch the fish and beans. Dried fish, it'll have to be.'

'That'll do very nicely.' The Tortoise looked satisfied and he cut away the thongs. As soon as he was free, the Lion hurried off and Kamba turned to the Chameleon.

'I am glad you came along,' he said, 'and very grateful to you. Where were you hiding?'

'I wasn't hiding,' answered Nadzikambe indignantly. 'I was dozing in a clump of fern when you came and hid that fine fat fish close by. Well, the fish, of course, soon began to attract the flies. I've had a delightful morning —never a dull moment, and such a wonderful breakfast! I hope I am going to have a wonderful supper, too.' The Chameleon cocked an inquiring eye at the Tortoise. 'You are going to invite me to your party, aren't you?'

'Yes, indeed,' said Kamba. 'You, and your *bangwe*. I shall, of course,' he added, with delicious malice, 'expect you to sing for your supper!'

THE OSTRICH AND THE CROCODILE

'WHAT's the matter with you?'

Kalulu, the Rabbit, was sitting, miserably, with his head between his paws and Nadzikambe, the Chameleon, eyed him with concern. 'You couldn't look more wretched if you'd got toothache!'

'That's just what I have got,' said Kalulu in a gloomy voice. 'Or maybe it's a fish-bone that's got stuck.'

'Have it out,' advised the Chameleon cheerfully.

'Much better have it out—only be sure you ask someone sensible to pull it for you. Don't ask the Ostrich! Ha! ha! ha!' Nadzikambe laughed at his little joke, and Kalulu looked sourly at him.

'I don't know what's so funny about that,' he said. 'Why shouldn't I ask the Ostrich? Not that I'd want to,' he added. 'Nthiwatiwa is so silly.'

'Just so,' agreed the Chameleon. 'But surely you know the old tale of the Ostrich and the Crocodile?'

Kalulu shook his head. 'No, but I see you mean to tell it to me, and I dare say it will take my mind off my aching jaw.' He didn't sound very optimistic.

'Nothing like a good story to cheer one up, I always say!' Nadzikambe himself loved either to tell or listen to a tale.

'So long as it *is* a good story. . . .'

'You must remember,' said Nadzikambe, ignoring the Rabbit's remark, 'that this is a tale of the days when the Ostrich's neck was no longer than that of any other bird: the days when Ostriches lived near the river and made their nests on sandbanks, in much the same way as the Crocodiles still do: the days when . . .' The Chameleon was off.

Spring was in the air. Everywhere the trees were bursting into leaf in shades of purple, lime and rust. The wild plums looked as if a host of small white clouds had fallen from the sky, the cassias bloomed as if it had been raining gold. All the birds had donned their bravest plumage and were carolling with joy as they set about the task of building nests.

On a sandbank by the river a pair of young Ostriches stood proudly by a hollow in the sand, gazing at their enormous eggs.

'Ten times bigger than that Crocodile's eggs!' The grey hen Ostrich gave a superior sniff and nodded her head towards the spot, not far away, where Ngwina, the Crocodile, had laid her eggs.

'Well, seven times, perhaps,' said her husband, who liked to be accurate.

'Fancy a great big creature like that laying such puny little eggs. And she doesn't even sit on them herself!'

'Very slack,' agreed the black Ostrich. 'Though, mind you, there is something to be said for her way of doing things—just covering the eggs with sand and letting the sun keep them warm. Very ingenious, you know. Very convenient.'

'And how does the sun keep them warm at night, I'd like to know?'

'Er . . . well, yes, I've been wondering about that.' And indeed this was true, for the black Ostrich, who always sat on the eggs himself at night, found it a very tedious business, as well as far from comfortable and, privately, he was more than a little envious of the Crocodile's method. 'You don't think we might try it ourselves?' he suggested suddenly.

His wife looked horrified. 'What!' she exclaimed. 'Desert our precious eggs? Let them get cold? I don't know what you can be thinking of!'

'Well, you were only saying yesterday how much you wished we could visit my brother's wife and see how many eggs she'd laid. If we covered ours over, like the

Crocodile, we could go. I'd like to see my brother again. It would be a nice change.'

The grey Ostrich looked at her husband in silence while she turned the matter over in her mind. She certainly did wish she knew about those other eggs—how many there were, when they were due to hatch—but dare she risk her own? She shook her head doubtfully. 'How do we know those Crocodile eggs will hatch?' she asked. 'They may have got cold. All that neglect!' She again sniffed virtuously.

At that moment a faint hiccupping sound could be heard coming from where the Crocodile's eggs lay buried. Immediately there was a commotion in the reeds and a huge grey-green Crocodile crawled out, her bright eyes gleaming with excitement as she rushed towards the eggs.

'Ah! My little treasures!' she cried. 'Come on out of your shells. Come along! Fight your way out and Mother will lead you to the water!' With her great claws, Ngwina swept the sand to one side: the hiccupping sounds became louder, the eggs began to rock and to crack and, from one after another, a little baby Crocodile emerged.

Fascinated, the Ostriches looked on. Then they turned to each other. 'You see?' said the black Ostrich. 'It's all right!'

The grey hen nodded. 'Yes. They have hatched. It must be all right!'

They looked again at the baby Crocodiles, who were now swimming gaily in the river, then smiled at each other and began to sweep the hot sand over their own eggs.

Night had fallen. Across the sky rolled ominous dark clouds, their edges silvered by a rising moon. The earth lay swathed in mystery. Beneath a spangled veil of dew, the tall reeds whispered as they guarded their sinister secrets. Like shadows, the Black-backed Jackals prowled the sandbanks, searching for their favourite supper—eggs.

They found the broken shells from which the baby Crocodiles had hatched, and a howl of disappointment splintered the night air. 'We are too late! Too late!' Stamping with rage, they ran to and fro, kicking at the sand, scratching and scrabbling, in the hope that another, later nest of eggs might be revealed. Suddenly, one Jackal's paw struck something hard and smooth and rounded, something like an egg but far, far bigger than any egg he'd ever found before. He investigated it. Oh, joy! It was an egg! Quickly he uncovered another and another, egg after egg—giant eggs! Eggs to dream of! Eggs to eat!

With whoops of delight the Jackals fell upon them. So hard were the shells that they could not break them open, until they discovered that if you rolled an egg to the rim of the nest and let it fall back against another, sooner or later it would crack and then, oh, my! What a feast it provided!

Long before the dawn broke, the Jackals had eaten their fill and were creeping home to rest and sleep and, maybe, dream about their glorious raid. The Owl and the Nightjar saw them go; sunrise showed the Heron the wreckage on the sandbank; the earliest Bees flew by and, buzzing with consternation, they raced off with the news. Rumour flared and spread like a bush-fire.

'Have you heard? The Ostriches left their nest and went off to visit their relations!'

'They say the Black-backed Jackals came and gorged themselves on Ostrich eggs until they could scarcely creep back home. . . .'

'They say the Crocodile's eggs hatched out before the raid. . . .'

'That's a pity!'

'They say Ngwina, the Crocodile, looks more smug and self-satisfied than ever!'

And then another rumour met and joined the first:

'Have you heard? The Ostriches are missing! They never reached their brother's nest. . . .'

'Lions were abroad last night.'

'They say the Lions dined off Ostriches. . . .'

'It was a hunters' night all right!'

'How foolish of the Ostriches to leave their eggs. It is different for Crocodiles, besides they lay so many. . . .'

'And who minds if all *their* eggs are destroyed. Nobody likes Crocodiles!'

'They say that all the Ostrich eggs were eaten. . . .'

'How very sad.'

But 'they' were not entirely right. One egg remained intact. It lay, still covered by a little sand, beneath the heap of broken shells. No one would have guessed that it was there. The hot sun warmed the sand by day, the sand retained sufficient warmth at night and, under its strange blanket, the egg lay safe and snug.

Day followed day. At length, one morning, when the youngest baby Crocodile, Ng'ona, lay basking on the sand, he was surprised to hear a tapping sound close by, *khu-khu-khu.* He cocked his horny little head on one side and listened carefully.

'Help me out!' a faint voice squeaked. 'Help me out!'

With a feeling of excitement, Ng'ona hastened to clear the debris and sweep away the sand and, just as he uncovered the egg, it cracked and out stepped the oddest-looking chick. It was covered with straw-coloured fluff and queer black bristles. Its head looked like some ridiculous pin-cushion and it had a large wide beak and, oh, such a sad expression! Ng'ona thought that never, in all his short life, had he seen anything so funny, and he began to laugh.

The chick blinked and gazed at the great big world around him. 'Who are you?' it lisped, when it saw the little Crocodile. 'Are you my bruvver?'

'No. I am Ng'ona,' replied the Crocodile. 'I've got lots of brothers and sisters, but they don't look anything like you. I don't think they are funny, but you are!' Ng'ona laughed so much that he started to roll down the bank. He reached the water's edge, had an idea and crawled back again. 'You've got no brothers or sisters,' he giggled, 'so I will be a brother to you. I will show you around.' Ng'ona had decided that it would be amusing to have the chick to play with instead of his own relations, who were always so disagreeable and bad-tempered, always fighting, always thinking of food. 'Have you got a name?' he asked. 'What shall I call you?'

'I've no idea,' replied the chick.

'But you must have a name. . . .'

'Nthiwatiwa was his father's name.'

At the sound of his mother's voice, Ng'ona jumped.

He supposed she wanted him for something or other. What a nuisance! Just as he was enjoying himself!

'Time you went swimming and caught yourself some fish,' she reminded her child. 'Your brothers and sisters are doing very well, and I can't think why you waste so much time, idling on the sandbank. Come along!' The great grey-green creature swirled her tail round and slid back into the water.

'I know. I'll call you 'Tiwa, for short! Come and swim with me,' Ng'ona called out, as he turned to follow his mother. But the little Ostrich shook his head. The world was a bewildering place, he thought, and he didn't like the look of the water and was sure he could not swim. He nestled into the warm sand, closed his eyes and, by the time that Ng'ona had submerged, Nthiwatiwa was fast asleep.

Days passed, weeks passed, months passed. The Ostrich and the Crocodile grew up and, despite the gloomy forebodings of neighbours, they remained good friends.

'Never trust a Crocodile,' the Pelican would say to 'Tiwa. 'Why, they can't even trust themselves! Sooner or later, he'll suddenly feel hungry and he'll eat you up. You mark my words.'

'I don't believe it,' the Ostrich would reply. 'Ng'ona wouldn't do a thing like that—he's my friend, my brother.'

'Huh!' snorted the Pelican. 'Crocodiles often eat their brothers, so just you take care!'

And the Crocodile's brothers and sisters would taunt

Ng'ona and call him names. 'Call yourself a Crocodile,' they'd sneer. 'Why, you are nothing but a lily-livered Lizard! Why don't you eat that stupid bird? He's fat enough, isn't he? If you don't eat him soon, one of us will gobble him up and then you'll look as silly as he does!' And Ng'ona would say: 'You leave 'Tiwa alone. He's *my* friend, so just you keep away from him!'

Then, one day, when there had been no rain for a long time and the river was low and fish were getting scarce, 'Tiwa, the Ostrich, found the Crocodile lying half in, half out of the water. Ng'ona was looking thin and very sorry for himself.

'Hallo!' said 'Tiwa anxiously. 'What's wrong? What's the matter with you?'

'I've got toothache,' the Crocodile answered miserably. 'Or maybe it's a fish-bone that's got stuck. Have a look in my mouth and pull it out, will you?' And Ng'ona opened his jaws as wide as they would go.

'Where does it hurt most?' 'Tiwa asked. 'Here?' He put his head into the Crocodile's mouth and tapped with his beak at an ugly-looking tooth.

'No, far'her bac'.' Ng'ona indicated the place as best he could. So 'Tiwa put his head still farther inside and, just as he was saying: 'Ah! This must be it!' Ng'ona suddenly felt hungry and closed his jaws, but, because the Ostrich's head was tough and leathery and so very far inside, Ng'ona couldn't close them properly and, automatically, he began to pull the Ostrich towards the river. Meanwhile, 'Tiwa had got a firm grip on what he supposed to be the offending tooth and he started to pull with all his might in the opposite direction. He pulled, the Crocodile pulled, and 'Tiwa's neck began to lengthen. It grew longer and longer. Still he pulled and the Crocodile pulled, then, suddenly, *plonk!* Out came the tooth!

With a yell of dismay, Ng'ona opened his jaws and flopped back into the water, while Nthiwatiwa staggered on to the bank, proudly holding the tooth in his beak. 'Here it is!' He beamed with delight as he placed the tooth on the sand.

'You blundering idiot!' screeched the Crocodile. 'You've pulled my tooth out. It was the fish-bone that I wanted out!'

'How was I to know? You just said "pull it out".' 'Tiwa sounded aggrieved and a worried look replaced his beaming smile. Slowly, he turned his head from side to side, then reared it up and looked about him. It felt very peculiar, but he could see much farther than he ever had before. 'What's happened to me?' he asked, wonderingly. 'What's happened to my neck?'

'That Crocodile has pulled it out for you!' With a great flapping of wings, the Pelican waddled on to the sandbank. 'I saw it all,' she said, 'and if you ask me, that toothache business was just a ruse. Ng'ona meant to eat you all along. I warned you never to trust a Crocodile!'

'You and your great gossiping beak!' Ng'ona bellowed rudely. 'Now I'll eat you both!' He gave a bark of rage and lashed out with his tail, trying to sweep the two birds into the river. When this manœuvre failed, he dashed up the bank and charged at them.

'Run! Run for your life, 'Tiwa,' shouted the Pelican,

as she rose into the air. 'And, in future, take my advice and keep away from Crocodiles!'

'Indeed, I will,' the Ostrich cried and went racing off, over the sandbanks, in and out of the reeds, twisting, turning, swerving, with never a pause. On he ran and on. . . . At length he reached the sandy plains, far, far from the river, far from any Crocodiles—'Tiwa hoped he'd never see a Crocodile again—and that is where he and his descendants have lived ever since.

'So that's how the Ostrich got his neck, is it?' Kalulu pursed his lips as the Chameleon concluded his story. 'Just fancy! But the Pelican was right—never trust a Crocodile.'

'Never,' agreed Nadzikambe. 'And how is your toothache now?' he asked. 'Would you like me to have a look inside your mouth?'

'No, thank you,' said the Rabbit. 'My toothache has gone. It suddenly got better while you were telling your tale and I didn't like to interrupt. Anyway'—Kalulu paused and grinned at the Chameleon—'it's just as well. I'd hate you to get a long, long neck. Why, you'd look even funnier than an Ostrich!'

THE SECRET STORE

MFUKO, the Mole, sat in one of his underground galleries, wondering why honey was so scarce and where all the termites had got to. Termite relish was considered by many to be a great delicacy and, in the past, there was always plenty to be had. Now everything was scarce, and yet the Bees maintained that they were making just as much honey and the Ants said they laid as many eggs. Mfuko was thinking how very queer it was, when a faint cry made him prick up his ears.

'Help!' shrilled a distant voice. 'Help! Oh, someone, come and get me out of this trap!'

'A bird in trouble!' said Mole to himself and scuttled off to answer the call, but before he could tunnel to the surface, another sound reached him—the sound of footsteps, soft, padding footsteps—and Mfuko recognized the Serval's sinister tread. Mole stopped abruptly and stood, listening. A moment later, a nasty chuckle splintered the cool evening air.

'Aha! What do I see in my snare? Namazeze, the Swallow, if I am not mistaken,' Njusi was saying. 'How very fortunate!'

Namazeze! An old friend of Mole's! Mfuko drew in his breath sharply. Caught in one of the Serval's hateful traps, was he, poor bird? That meant, at best, that the Serval would take him prisoner and make him a slave—a terrible fate for a Swallow or, indeed, for anyone. Mfuko shut his eyes tightly, wrinkled his forehead, and tried to think of a way to rescue his friend. If only he knew where the Serval lived: what he did with his prisoners: where he kept his slaves? He wondered who would know? Nadzikambe, the Chameleon, perhaps? Yes, he might? Meanwhile, the Serval was speaking again and Mfuko strained his ears to hear what was being said.

'. . . and we'll just tie this rope round you so that I can guide you home—I wouldn't like you to lose your way, he! he! he!' Njusi laughed heartily at his joke. 'Then, in the morning, you'll be able to help me with my work. There is so much to do and I need a new potter badly. I am sure you will be good at making pots

—you make such clever nests, ha! ha! ha!' The Serval laughed again and Mfuko shuddered at the sound. He could not imagine why Njusi should need a potter, but he felt sure that Namazeze was in for a bad time, especially if he could not do the work required of him. There was no doubt that the Swallow would have to be rescued.

All this time Namazeze had said nothing, but, as the Serval dragged him from the trap and fastened the rope round his body, pinioning his wings, the Swallow gave one last shout for help.

'Dear, dear!' wheezed the Serval. 'How ungrateful some birds are! Fortunately there is no one to hear your cries and I can assure you that it will be much better for you if you learn to keep your beak shut. I can't bear birds who screech. They get on my nerves. So don't let us have any more noise or trouble—I'd hate to have to be rough with you.' The threatening note in Njusi's voice gave the lie to his words and Mfuko clenched his paws angrily as he muttered: 'The hypocrite! But he's wrong about one thing. Someone has heard Namazeze's cry. I have, and I am going to save my friend.' He wished there were some way of letting the Swallow know, but he dared not come to the surface while Njusi was about.

Minutes passed. The sound of retreating footsteps died away. Very cautiously, Mfuko tunnelled upwards, emerged above ground and hurried along the track that the Serval had taken. It led across the wooded slope of the mountain and into a little green valley that ended in a dark and gloomy gully. From the number of trees that

had been felled, it looked as if someone had been building a house near by. The Serval, perhaps? Very likely, Mole thought, and if that were so, maybe he'd be wise to get below again. There was little sense in going on, for it was almost dark and Njusi and his captive could not be far away. Besides, the track vanished amongst the rocks of the gully, where no doubt the Serval had his lair, and Mfuko did not want to venture there. Rocks, in his opinion, were very unsatisfactory terrain—you could not go to ground just as you liked, and secret passages took a lot of making. No, he decided, for the present, at any rate, he'd keep clear of the gully and get busy on an underground runway from the valley and, in the morning, he would look for the Chameleon and find out if he knew anything about the Serval and his ways.

Taking care to leave as little trace of his visit as possible, Mfuko tunnelled down into the soft earth. Soon, a fine new passage was under construction.

Green as the arum-lily leaf on which he was sitting, Nadzikambe, the Chameleon, resembled nothing so much as an absurd small dragon. A happy dragon, for the sun was shining, he had breakfasted well, and the day promised to be a glorious one—the sort of day, in fact, on which to make music, sing songs and laugh at life.

Nadzikambe picked up his *bangwe* and played a gay little tune, and he was just going to burst into song when a flurry of earth caused him to pause and swivel an eye in the direction of the disturbance. A moment later, Mole's muddied nose came thrusting through the loosened soil. The Chameleon greeted him with a shout of joy.

'Mfuko! How delightful! How are you, old fellow? What a long time it is since last we met!'

'Yes, indeed,' agreed the Mole, blinking his little eyes in the unaccustomed sunlight. 'And I want to see you most particularly. How lucky it was that you were playing your *bangwe*—it made it so much easier for me to find you. I could hear you from a long way off.'

'You have such wonderful hearing,' Nadzikambe said. 'But I should have been singing. You'd have heard me for miles then! And if I'd known you were coming, I'd have sung a digging song, especially for you. Like this:

Mole
is digging
in the deep
dark
earth.

Mole
is digging
a long
dark
path.

Mole
is scuttling
down the long
dark
way.

Mole
is tunnelling
to the
sunlit
day.

Mfuko beamed with pleasure and both he and the Chameleon laughed. Then becoming serious, the Mole told Nadzikambe about his friend, the Swallow, and of all that had happened on the previous day.

'Can you help me?' Mfuko asked, anxiously. 'Do you know what Njusi does with his victims? He is so mean and wicked that I am sure he ill-treats them.'

'I shouldn't wonder,' agreed the Chameleon. 'No one ever goes to his dark gully and nobody knows what happens there. Even the birds and the bees avoid it.' Nadzikambe was silent for a full minute, then he took a deep breath. 'Shall I go and explore it and see if I can find Namazeze? I think I could go without being seen.'

'Oh! Would you? Could you? It would be a very brave thing to do.' Mole's voice was full of admiration. 'If you find Namazeze, tell him we are going to rescue him. It will cheer and comfort him to know that. I know!' Mfuko went on, excitedly. 'I'll take you along my new passage and, while you explore the rocks, I will see how far I can tunnel under them. There is an old burrow of Antbear's near by where we can meet.'

Full of hopeful plans, the two friends set off on their bold adventure. When they reached the Antbear's burrow, they parted company, agreeing to meet again, if possible at noon, and anyway by one hour after sunset.

The Chameleon crawled upwards, changed his colour from earthy-red to rock-grey and, in next to no time, became invisible amongst the ancient boulders. Mfuko, the Mole, paused for a while to listen for any interesting sounds that might reach him, but, hearing none, he set about tunnelling as hard as he could go. Very quickly he got to the rocks and bored down into the earth, searching for a passage under them. He worked fast, found the going easier than he dared hope and, whenever a seam of earth permitted, he tunnelled upwards again, so as to be able to hear anything of significance that might be going on above the surface of the ground.

For a long time there was nothing unusual, but at length an odd little noise reached him, a sort of scratching noise such as a bird might make by tapping on rock with his claw. Mole wondered if it could be the Swallow and found his heart beating with excitement as he worked his way towards the sound. Very cautiously he bored along but, after a short distance, he was brought to a standstill by a wall of stakes that had been driven into the ground. They seemed to form a semicircle, built out from the rock. Mfuko tried to puzzle out their meaning. Were they part of some dwelling—a prison, for instance? He listened intently, but the scratching had ceased and he could detect no sound of movement anywhere near. He decided to burrow under the stakes and look for some suitable place to surface. He felt he must know what the structure was and what lay inside.

Down he sank again into the earth, down, down, down . . . under the stakes . . . then up once more . . . up . . . a pause to make certain that it was safe to emerge . . . one more upwards thrust and his head was popping out of the ground.

It was very still inside the building and little light filtered through. Mfuko was glad, for he could see better in the dark. With only his head and shoulders visible, he looked around and gave a low whistle of surprise. Everywhere there were pots and jars—on shelves, on ledges of the rock, even on the ground. Pots of all kinds, jars of all shapes. Evidently the place was a storehouse. Mfuko came right out of his hole and examined the nearest jar. It was full to the brim with honey. So was the next jar, and the next. This, then, was where all the honey had got to, was it? Into this secret storehouse of the Serval's? Mfuko was sure it was the Serval's. Hadn't Njusi told the Swallow that he needed pots? And for what other purpose could he need so many? Mole wondered what the pots contained and hurriedly examined one. Termite relish? He rubbed a paw against his velvet coat to clean it, dipped a claw into the pot and had a taste. Yes, termite relish, it was. Absolutely delicious!

He was just going to scoop out another claw-full, when he heard the scratching noise again. It seemed to come from somewhere high up in the rock, somewhere outside the actual storehouse. Well, if Namazeze was imprisoned up there, there was little that Mole could do, but maybe the Chameleon could reach him. In any case, Mfuko decided, it was time to return to the Antbear's burrow. With the utmost care, he flattened the earth that he had disturbed, moved a jar or two to screen the entrance to his passage, then hurried back by the way that he had come.

There was no sign of the Chameleon when he reached the burrow. In a fever of impatience, Mfuko waited for him to appear. He had luncheon, attempted to sleep, found he could not do so, so took to pacing restlessly up and down, trying to think of a way to rescue the Swallow. At last the sun went down and Mfuko heard a slight movement. He turned his head, and there, beside him, was Nadzikambe.

'Well?' he asked eagerly. 'What luck?'

'I've found him,' the Chameleon said. 'At least, I know where he is imprisoned. It is not going to be easy to rescue him, I fear. What luck have you had?'

The Mole told him.

'Oho! A secret storehouse!' Nadzikambe's voice rose in an excited squeak. 'So that's what the building below Namazeze's prison is. I wondered what it could be. There is a sort of cave in the rock above it, where Namazeze sits in a cage, making pots. I could not speak to him because the Serval was there.'

'Poor Namazeze.' Mfuko gave a deep sigh. 'While I've been waiting for you,' he went on, 'I've been thinking—thinking hard. And the conclusion I have come to is this. We must find a magic that will make the Serval set the Swallow free.'

'That's an idea!' The Chameleon clasped his forepaws together in his enthusiasm. 'There is an old proverb isn't there: "If the Msuku tree does not drop its fruit, you shake it"?'

'Yes.'

'And what we want is a magic to "shake" Njusi.'

'Yes. If we can make him think that he has been

bewitched and that the Swallow is the cause, he'll be only too thankful to let Namazeze go.'

'Of course he will.' For some minutes the Chameleon sat deep in thought. Then he jumped up excitedly. 'What we must do is this: first of all, we must create a disturbance that will lure the Serval away from the cave. You will have to manage that. I will hide myself as near to the Swallow as I can and, as soon as Njusi is out of the way, I will tell Namazeze our plans. I must get some feathers from him—we must have feathers to make a proper magic—feathers, and a few Serval hairs. There'll be plenty of those lying about, I expect. Then we can get into the storehouse by your tunnel and bewitch the pots. . . .' Nadzikambe began to laugh. 'Oh, what fun this is going to be,' he chuckled in a sudden ecstasy of merriment.

Mfuko grinned at him. 'I do believe it is,' he said. 'Now, let's make sure we know exactly what we are going to do. . . .'

Strange things were happening in the dark gully where the Serval lived. In broad daylight, a pot of honey had suddenly leapt out of the ground and smashed itself to pieces before Njusi's very own eyes. He had been so amazed that he had left his captive to go and investigate the matter. He was away for quite a long time, but could find no satisfactory explanation of the phenomenon. Feeling more than a little worried, he returned to the cave, only to be greeted at the entrance by a sinister omen—a charm made of poison berries, swallow feathers and three Serval hairs. It was hanging upside-down and

there was no mistaking its message. He looked at it and his eyes narrowed wickedly.

'Who put that there?' he demanded. 'Who has been here while I have been away?'

'The Spirits of my Ancestors,' replied the Swallow. 'They do not like the way you are treating me. They wish you to set me free.'

'That I will not do.' Njusi snarled and angrily told the Swallow to get on with his work. He went back to the charm and stared at it. He reached up, then stopped. A terrible thought had come into his head. Perhaps it contained some dreadful poison and if he were to touch it . . .? He shuddered and turned hurriedly away.

Resolutely putting the charm out of his mind, he walked round feverishly, trying to puzzle out the mystery of the jar of honey. How could that have happened unless the thing had been bewitched? Where had the honey pot come from? Goodness! Not from his own store? He halted, appalled at the thought, and the more he considered the matter, the more obvious it became that that was precisely where it had come from. In a frenzy, he dashed off to have a look at the storehouse.

His heart was thumping uncomfortably as he approached, and it missed a beat altogether when he saw what was hanging over the entrance. Another omen, similar to the one at the cave, but this contained an Owl's feather—the direct warning that any wrong that had been done must be righted. He looked at it, fearfully at first, then with defiance as he boldly pushed open the door. . . .

The screech of rage that escaped him, when he saw

that more than half his precious pots and jars had vanished, died to a frozen silence as one jar began to move towards him of its own accord. Spell-bound, Njusi gazed at it. Then, from the depths of the jar, a strange, unearthly voice started to sing:

He,
who robs
a bird of freedom,
shall,
himself,
be robbed.

SET THE SWALLOW FREE!

He,
who robs
the Bees of honey,
shall,
himself,
be robbed.

SET THE SWALLOW FREE!!

He,
who steals
the termite relish,
shall,
himself,
be robbed.

SET THE SWALLOW FREE!!!

The song ended and the jar began to rock to and fro.

Suddenly the ground beneath the Serval trembled and, for one awful moment, Njusi thought he was falling—falling into some horrible, bottomless pit. With a tremendous effort, he pulled himself together and leapt for the door. Without a single backward glance, he dashed to the cave and, with shaking paws, unfastened the bars of Namazeze's cage.

'Go!' hissed the Serval, in a terrified whisper. 'Go, at once, and leave me in peace. Tell your Ancestors to take away their spells. Tell them they can have my jars and pots. Go!'

Namazeze needed no second bidding. With a joyous burst of song, he ran to the entrance of the cave, spread his wings and flew away.

A shaft of moonlight illuminated the Antbear's burrow, where the three friends were having supper. It had been an exhausting day. Most of the jars and pots from the Serval's secret hoard had been handed over to the Chief for distribution amongst his people. Some had been left in the store for Njusi's own use. Some remained in the burrow and, of these, more than a few were now empty.

'I feel sick,' announced Nadzikambe, the Chameleon, in a sticky voice. 'It's all that rocking about in empty honey jars.'

'Huh!' said the Mole with a grin. 'That's not the cause. You've had too much honey and too much termite relish!'

'Nonsense,' mumbled the Swallow, with his mouth full. 'Don't be absurd. As if one could have too much termite relish!' he said, blissfully reaching for yet another pot of the delicious stuff.

THE RITUAL COMING-OF-AGE

A WHITE sun blazed in the noonday sky. As the land wilted in the shimmering haze of heat, the village Goats lay chewing drowsily in any patch of shade that offered, their minds as empty as their mouths were full. A few hens scratched in the dust and on the rubbish heap. Overhead, a Hawk hovered like a sentinel keeping watch on anything that moved.

Nadzikambe, the Chameleon, eyed the Hawk thoughtfully. 'Those poor, silly hens!' he sighed. 'They've looked for it for so many generations, I doubt if they know what they are searching for now.'

'Well, what are they searching for?' asked a young Gecko. 'Please tell me what "it" is.'

'Do you mean to say you do not know?' The Chameleon was surprised at such ignorance, but he was also delighted because he would now be able to amuse himself by telling the story to the little blue-tailed Lizard.

'The events that I am about to relate,' Nadzikambe began rather pompously, 'took place a long, long time ago. . . .'

For three days there had been great rejoicing in the village of Chief Mbalame, where the coming-of-age of his daughter had been celebrated with traditional ceremony. Beer had been brewed and gleefully consumed; instruction in all matters had been given; the girl had received the ritual hair-cut, been smeared with oil, adorned with brightly coloured beads. The final dance had ended and the drums had ceased to beat. Save for the clucking of Mkota, the Hen, all was quiet again in the little village on the hill.

Mkota, the Hen, had plenty to say, for she, too, had a daughter, Nkhuku, who was soon to come of age and she saw no reason why the occasion should not be observed with similar pomp and ceremony. Was she not the Chieftain's oldest and most valued hen? Surely it was only right and proper that her daughter should come of age in style? She said so to her sister, Nyole.

'Are not our children the daughters of Chiefs?'

'Indeed they are,' the sister replied with a proud look towards the rock where Tambala, the Cock, stood flapping his wings as he proclaimed, in his strident voice, that he was Chief of all the Birds.

'Very well, then,' said Mkota, 'we must decide what things are wanted and where they are to be found. . . .'

'And whom we shall invite to attend the ceremony. . . .'

'Of course. But one thing at a time. Now, what is the most important item?'

'Beer,' prompted a cockerel, who was giving himself a dust bath close by.

The two hens frowned at him. 'Impertinence!' said Mkota. 'Beer is not the most important item and this matter is no concern of yours.'

'Mind you,' Nyole lowered her voice a little, 'he's right. We must have beer.'

'Of course we must have beer,' agreed Mkota, 'but beer is easy to get. There is still plenty to be had in the village. And oil—that can be made from sesame seeds.'

'Beads?' queried Nyole. 'Where can we get beads?'

'Pawpaw seeds.'

'Wouldn't pumpkin seeds be better?'

'Or berries? Any of them would do very well.'

'No trouble about beads, then. The ritual cut? Where can we find a cutter that will cut feathers? You tell me that,' Nyole demanded.

'Where indeed!' The two hens clucked gently, turning the problem over in their minds. They knew they could not hope to borrow the tribal cutter—anyway, that only cut hair—no, they needed a special cutter. Surely some bird owned one? But who? They asked each other, who would know?

'Nkhunda may be able to help us.' As the little grey

Dove came flying down, the hens greeted her effusively and lost no time in telling her their plans for Nkhuku's coming-of-age.

'You know the birds in the forest,' said Mkota. 'Which of them, do you suppose, would have a cutter?'

'Mkuwi, the Eagle,' the Dove answered promptly. 'He is sure to have one. He has everything.'

'Do you think he would lend it to us?'

The Dove looked a little doubtful. 'Well, I don't know. . . .'

'Would you go and ask him? Please ask him for us, Nkhunda. I'm sure he would do anything for you,' begged one hen, and the sister added her quota of flattery: 'You could persuade him, Nkhunda, if anybody could!'

'Perhaps. I suppose I could try. But it is a long way to go'—the Dove was thinking aloud—'and I don't like the look of the weather.'

The birds lifted their heads to gaze at the sky which had begun the day with such bright promise. Now, the early azure was hidden behind clouds: the beautiful, deceitful clouds whose sunlit whiteness turns to grey, the grey to indigo: clouds that can spell thunder, lightning, rain.

'It won't come to anything,' Mkota predicted, determined that it shouldn't, and Nyole said, hopefully: 'Not more than a shower, I'd say.'

'I wouldn't be so sure,' murmured the Dove with a shake of her head. 'But, since you are so anxious to have the cutter, I will see what I can do.'

'Oh, you are a dear, kind creature, Nkhunda!'

exclaimed the two hens, cackling with delight. 'We shall never be able to thank you enough.'

'If all goes well, I should be back tomorrow evening.' The grey Dove spread her wings and the hens watched her flight until the great trees of the forest hid her from their sight.

All afternoon the thunder rolled amongst the hills, but no rain fell; at night the moonless sky was lit by sudden flashes. Beyond the mountain, a storm broke and spent itself in violence, but, by morning, all was calm and bright again, until the white clouds piled up in renewal of their threat.

The village hens were in a state of feverish excitement. They fussed about, collecting pots or beer and sesame oil, seeds for beads, ants' eggs, grain and green food, all the most delicious titbits they could find, and all the time they clucked incessantly. Again and again they discussed their plans and which guests should be invited. Again and again they wondered how the Dove was faring. Had she found the Eagle? Had she been able to persuade Mkuwi to lend his cutter? How soon could they look for her return? From time to time they would gaze towards the thickly wooded mountains, hoping the little grey Dove might come flying back sooner than she had expected. The mountains now lay in a patchwork of shadow and sunshine, dark purplish patches from the shadow of the clouds, chequered with the sunlit green of trees, and over the forest a thin grey veil of rain had fallen from the sky. A rainbow formed and, as the hens stood gazing at its beauty, a little bird came flying through the arc.

'Look! Look!' cried Mkota, excitedly.

'Where?' asked her sister, and then she saw the Dove. 'It's Nkhunda!' she clucked. 'It must be. Has she got the cutter?'

'Surely she is carrying something in her beak?'

'Yes. Yes, she is!' The two hens cackled hysterically as the Dove flew down and laid the precious cutter on the ground. Mkota pounced on it immediately, picked it up, examined the little razor-like object, tested its edge and nearly cut her claw, it was so sharp, then turned to thank Nkhunda.

The Dove was weary but looking strangely beautiful. Her feathers had a sheen they had not known before, her breast had taken on a pinkish tinge, as if the rainbow through which she'd passed had given her a little of its colour. When she had rested a while, Nkhunda began to tell the hens of her adventures.

She had found the Eagle and his mate, standing by a leaf-lined nest of sticks, gazing fondly at their fluffy chick. So proud they were, so haughty and so grand, Nkhunda had scarcely dared approach, but she had summoned up sufficient courage and, once the courtesies had been observed, she had laid the hens' request before the Eagles, as the request of one Chief's family to another. The Eagles seemed impressed. Pomp and ceremony appealed to them, but the cutter was a priceless treasure. If they were to lend it, they feared it might get lost.

'It was not easy to persuade them that their cutter would be safe,' Nkhunda told the hens. 'I promised that you'd take the greatest care.'

'We will. Of course we will,' the hens affirmed. 'As if we'd be so careless as to lose a thing like that. The idea!'

'You can be sure it will be safe with us,' said Nyole confidently.

'The Eagle's anger would be great if it were lost,' Nkhunda almost sounded scared, 'so guard the cutter well.'

'We will.'

'Of course we will!'

A garden, from which the millet had been harvested, had been chosen as the scene of the celebrations for Nkhuku's coming-of-age. The village hens and all their guests had gathered there. They had feasted, they had danced, the early rites had been performed and now the ceremony had reached its climax, as the Chicken's head and neck were shorn of feathers. Excitement mounted, the dance grew wilder and wilder and Mkota and her sister became more and more elated. Never before had any hen's daughter come of age in such magnificent style. This was an occasion that would be long remembered!

The dance continued. Every now and then, a hen would fall out and bustle round, fetching this, removing that, refilling pots, emptying baskets. The shorn feathers were swept up and thrown upon the village refuse heap, a broken pot was buried in a hole in the ground. And still the dance went on. It went on until, one after another, the weary fowls sank exhausted to the earth and fell asleep where they lay. The weary guests departed, vowing that the coming-of-age had been a real triumph.

At length, silence reigned once more.

Mkota slept peacefully for some time, then she began to dream. She dreamed she saw a dark half-moon wheeling in the sky, a giant bird that soared above, casting its shadow on the earth below. It sailed round and round, in ever diminishing circles, hovered an instant, hung motionless, then plunged into a headlong dive and came to rest upon a near-by rock. Mkota could see the great bird clearly, its haughty, crested head with the cruel, curving beak; the short ash-coloured tail; its glistening feathers, black as the night, a hint of chestnut, white beneath the wings; the orange legs and talons, such cruel, curving talons! A fierce, accusing eye was fixed upon her as the Eagle raised one claw and pointed straight at her. . . .

'The cutter! Where is the cutter?'

With a squawk of alarm, Mkota awoke to find her sister, Nyole, pecking at her in agitation. 'Have you got the cutter?' she demanded. 'Where is it?'

Mkota scrambled to her feet. 'The cutter!' she screeched, fluffing up her feathers. 'I gave it to you. Haven't you got it?'

'I gave it back to you.'

'When?'

'When the feathers were shorn.'

'But I gave it to you to hold.'

'You didn't.'

'I did. I know I did.'

'I don't remember it.'

'Well, never mind that. We must find it.'

'Yes.'

The two hens ran to the spot where the ritual cutting had taken place and began their search. They searched everywhere, every inch of the ground. There was no sign of the cutter.

'Who cleared away the debris?' Mkota asked. 'It must have been swept up with the feathers.'

'I don't know,' replied Nyole. 'Let's go and search the refuse heap.'

They ran to it, they searched frantically, they scratched over the whole area, but still there was no sign of the cutter. They ran back to the scene of the dance, roused all the sleeping fowls. 'The Eagle's cutter has been lost. Wake up! Wake up! Search for it. Search everywhere. It must be found!'

The fowls woke, cackled their protests at being disturbed, clucked with annoyance, but they, too, joined in the search. No one could remember having seen the cutter. With all the excitement there had been, it was not surprising it had got mislaid, but, as they all agreed, it must be somewhere! It was just a matter of searching. . . .

'And,' said Nadzikambe, the Chameleon, 'they have been searching for it ever since. The cutter has never been found.'

'Were the Eagles very angry?' asked the Gecko, with one eye on a gnat that was whining around.

'They were furious. They have never forgiven the hens. See that old Kabawe up there?' The Chameleon pointed at the Hawk who was still hovering over the village. 'They say the Eagle sends him to see that the

Chickens do not give up the search. From time to time the Hawk, or even Mkuwi himself, will seize a Chicken in payment for the cutter. They take a heavy toll, but there is no end to the feud, nor ever will be until the cutter is found. Excuse me. . . .' The Chameleon broke off as the gnat came within range. Two tongues darted out simultaneously.

'My gnat, I think,' said Nadzikambe, with a happy smile. 'What an advantage it is to have a long tongue!'

THE JACKAL AND THE FIG TREE

A Fig Tree,
A Fig Tree!
Where can I find
A Fig Tree?

So sang the furry little Jackal, as he played a game of his own invention with plum stones and a green bush orange. The season of plums was over, the bush orange had tasted as bitter as usual and Nkhandwe, who dearly loved to eat fruit, was wishing that he knew of a fig tree, because it was just the time when figs should be at their best. The only tree he'd been able to find had a very poor crop and most of the figs were riddled with ants and were not worth eating. It was very disappointing.

A shadow passed over the clearing where the little Jackal was playing and Nkhandwe looked up into the cloudless sky to see what had caused it. Well, thought he, bless my paws and whiskers, what an extraordinary sight! Two Crows carrying a basket made of plaited reeds! The basket appeared to have two handles through which a thin stick of bamboo had been thrust. Each Crow had one end of the bamboo in its beak and the basket hung between them.

Nkhandwe thought this was very interesting and he wondered what was in the basket. The Crows wouldn't be carrying it for nothing, he reasoned. Either they were on their way to fill it—surely with something special—or it was already full. The matter was certainly worth investigating. The little Jackal watched the Crows until they settled on a tree. He marked the spot as best he could and made his way towards it. When he got close, he flattened himself and crept cautiously through the bushes until he was in a position to see what was going on.

The Crows were emptying the basket on to the ground. Out of it tumbled a heap of greenish-purple fruits. Figs! Figs! Figs! thought Nkhandwe and his mouth began to water. These clearly harboured no ants but were as luscious as all figs should be. Why—the Crows had begun to eat them—you could see the juice trickling out of their beaks! It was more than the little Jackal could endure. With absolutely no difficulty, he put on the pathetic, half-starved look that he had often found so useful, trotted out of the bushes and across the clearing, just as if he were a hungry little Jackal hunting vainly for his supper. He passed the Crows, apparently intent on his own business, halted suddenly and turned his head to look at them.

'Oh!' he breathed, with wistful eyes fixed on the figs. 'My favourite fruit!' The Crows took no notice of him at all. He sighed, moved on a few steps, stopped again and looked back. The Crows were stuffing themselves with figs just as fast as they could and the pile of fruit was dwindling rapidly.

'Boo-hoo-hoo!' The little Jackal burst into loud sobs and the Crows looked up.

'Wha's'h'matter?' asked Khungubwe, squelchily. The other Crow, Mpopo, said nothing. Her mouth was too full to speak.

'I'm so hungry,' sobbed the little Jackal. 'Where did you find those lovely figs? C-couldn't I find some, too?'

'You won't find our fig tree,' said Khungubwe, and went on eating.

Mpopo swallowed. 'Somewhere you can't get to,' she chuckled in a sneering sort of way. 'It's on an island, and you can't fly and you can't swim. Too bad, isn't it?'

An island? Nkhandwe reduced the volume of his sobs and did some quick thinking. Was there no way by which he could reach an island? Lucky Crows to be able to fly! Why, oh, why couldn't he? . . . Well, *why* couldn't he? Surely there was a way?

'Will you be going back to the island?' Nkhandwe asked.

'Of course.'

'When?'

'At cock-crow,' said Mpopo.

'At dawn,' said Khungubwe.

'Same thing,' said Mpopo. 'Anyway, it's no business of yours!'

'Couldn't you take me with you?' asked the little Jackal.

The Crows stared at him, amazed at the suggestion. 'Of course not,' they said. 'We aren't going to share our fig tree with anyone. Now, run along and stop bothering us. Here's a fig for you!' Khungubwe picked one up and tossed it across to the Jackal. It was a bit unripe but Nkhandwe enjoyed it. He said 'thank you' and trotted off. He had a good deal to do before nightfall.

First of all, he had to see Tambala, the Cock. The little Jackal felt sure that, for a handful of corn, Tambala would agree to wake much earlier than usual, and he was right. Next, he paid a call on Nadzikambe, the Chameleon. He knew that he could rely on the Chameleon for help and it was never difficult to start a fire when the grass was dry. Finally, he collected some reeds and plaited them into a little mat, a mat that would be just about the right size to fit into the Crows' basket.

The night was dark, dark as the Crows who slept so soundly in the dark tree in the forest. Below them stood their empty-looking basket. The bright stars winked at each other in the sapphire sky. Suddenly a cock began to crow: 'Wake up! Wake up! Day is breaking!' A little later, a faint red glow showed in the East, a glow such as heralds the dawn or proclaims a burning fire.

The Crows began to stir. 'What? Dawn already?' they muttered sleepily. The cock crowed again. 'Come on,' said the Crows, 'we'd better go. We don't want any other bird to reach the island before us.' They hopped down from the tree, groped around until they found the bamboo stick, thrust it through the handles of the basket and took the ends in their beaks, then rose into the air and flew straight out to the lake.

The Crows were over the water before it occurred to either of them that the basket seemed rather heavy for an empty one. They glanced at it out of the corners of their eyes, but, as far as they could see, it *was* empty. Not that anyone could see much, it was so dark. Surprisingly dark, considering dawn had broken. Each Crow wondered whether the other had noticed anything strange, but neither dared speak, for fear of losing the basket. They could not open their beaks and let go their hold on the bamboo, or the basket would fall into the lake. There was nothing for it but to keep on course.

They reached the island, flew to the fig tree and put the basket down on the ground. It was still dark and even the red glow had faded from the sky. The Crows were very puzzled. They did not know what to make of it at all. It was always light soon after cock-crow!

'I don't understand . . .' Khungubwe began.

'I don't like it!' said Mpopo.

'Why is the sun not up? It should be up by now.'

'Why is it so dark? The sun does not begin the day and then go back to sleep!'

'The basket seemed heavier than it should,' said Khungubwe. 'Did you not think so?'

'Yes.'

'Now, why should that be?'

Mpopo shook her head. 'Let us examine it,' she suggested.

They turned to the basket, peered into it, tipped it up. Something rolled out.

'Oh, my!' squawked Mpopo, with a startled jump.

'What is it?' croaked Khungubwe. They waited nervously to see if it showed any signs of life. When nothing happened, they plucked up enough courage to prod it, first with a claw, then with their beaks. It seemed to be a bit of wood. Dead wood from the tree, perhaps, that had somehow fallen in? That, of course, would explain it. They sighed with relief. The sky, at last, was growing pale and the Crows decided that they would have an early breakfast of figs and then fill up the basket with any that were left.

Nkhandwe, the Jackal, had already started on his breakfast of figs. Under cover of the thick, low branches of the tree, he was eating happily and chuckling with delight at the way in which his scheme had worked. Tambala and Nadzikambe had, evidently, done their part to perfection. Meanwhile, he had had a splendid night, asleep in the basket, beneath the little mat that he had made. The mat looked exactly like the bottom of the basket and only a very observant bird would have noticed the difference in depth, especially in the dark. As for the difference in weight, it had been simple enough to hop out as soon as the Crows had put the basket down and, while they were puzzling over the strangeness of the dawn, he'd been able to drop in the piece of broken branch. Nothing, really, could have been easier. The return journey might be more difficult, but for the present, thought Nkhandwe, everything was fine, especially the figs!

Khungubwe and Mpopo took a long time over their breakfast. So did the little Jackal, but once the Crows started on the job of filling up the basket, Nkhandwe became very much on the alert. He waited until the Crows were engrossed in gathering the figs from the far side of the tree, then, like a flash, he was in the basket and once more under his mat. The few figs already lying on it only helped in the deception, and soon more figs were being piled on top. It was not too uncomfortable but inclined to be hot and stuffy and the little Jackal began to feel drowsy. After a while, he found it impossible to keep awake.

When the basket was full, the Crows got ready for their flight, but, what with its weight and the number of figs they had eaten, they had some difficulty in taking off. After the second attempt had failed, Khungubwe stood and looked thoughtfully at the basket.

'We'll have to lighten the load,' he then announced, in a gloomy voice.

'Nonsense,' said Mpopo. 'We've managed a full basket before, so we can manage it again. You've eaten too much, that's what the trouble is!'

'Speak for yourself,' Khungubwe returned, indignantly. 'You've eaten just as much as I have.'

'Well, be that as it may'—Mpopo had, if anything, eaten rather more—'I am sure we can manage. Now, take hold of your end of the bamboo. . . .' Flapping wings, a few hops, a little run and . . . all was well! Away they sailed, out over the lake.

Curled up at the bottom of the basket, Nkhandwe, the Jackal, was having a nightmare. He was in an earthquake, trapped in a hole in the ground. Rocks and stones and earth were falling on him . . . he was being stifled . . . he must get out! In his sleep, he began to toss and turn and scrabble.

'Help! Help!' he yelped. 'Help me out! Help me out!'

'Caw!'

'Caw! Caw!'

The Crows were terrified at the extraordinary noise that was coming from the basket and, at the first startled croak, the bamboo fell from their beaks and the basket went hurtling down into the lake.

'Caw! Our basket!' croaked Khungubwe, flapping distractedly overhead.

'Our figs! We've lost them all!' wailed Mpopo.

'Whatever was that sound?'

'Who knows! The basket must have been bewitched!'

'Maybe we are well rid of it, then!'

'Maybe we are,' agreed Mpopo. The two Crows looked down to where the basket now floated on the water, surrounded by floating figs. A strange, bedraggled object clutched frantically at it. Goodness alone knew what the object was—a witch, perhaps? Scared out of their wits, the Crows looked hurriedly away and continued on their flight.

Ng'ona, the Crocodile, lay among the reeds, wondering what he should do. His child was sick and the Witch Doctor whom he had consulted had shaken his head and predicted that nothing but the heart of some four-footed, furry creature could cure her. And where, Ng'ona was asking himself, was he going to find a thing like that.

Overhead, a pair of Crows were making a good deal of noise, and something unusual appeared to have fallen into the lake. Ng'ona thought he might as well see what it was. He slid quietly under water and swam towards the place. Quietly he inspected what he found. From beneath the water, it seemed to be some flimsy sort of raft from which two wet and hairy legs were dangling. Even to a Crocodile, they did not look particularly appetizing. Ng'ona was about to swim back to the reeds when the thought occurred to him that wet, hairy legs would be furry legs, if they were dry. With considerable excitement, he wondered what the legs belonged to. Was it some two-footed creature or had it four feet? Cautiously, he raised himself until his eyes were just above the surface of the water . . . wonder of wonders! It was a four-footed, furry creature! That Witch Doctor was infallible! Now his child could be cured.

Ng'ona rose still farther out of the water and grinned at Nkhandwe. 'Hallo!' he said. 'You seem to be in trouble.'

Too true, thought Nkhandwe, but aloud he said: 'Please, will you ferry me back to the land? I will give you anything I have, if only you will take me safely to the shore.'

'Will you give me your heart?' asked the Crocodile.

'My heart?' The little Jackal blinked twice and swallowed. 'Why should you want my heart?' he asked, stalling for time, while he tried to work out some sort of plan.

'My child is sick and the heart of a four-footed, furry creature is the only medicine that will cure her.'

'Ah, yes,' said Nkhandwe, 'of course, there is no more powerful medicine than the heart of a Jackal. What a pity I have not got mine with me!'

'What do you mean?' asked Ng'ona. If the Jackal had not got his heart with him, then where was it?

'I never take my heart with me when I am travelling over water,' the little Jackal explained. 'I find it so much safer to leave it on land.'

'Where have you left it?' Ng'ona demanded. He was determined to have the Jackal's heart.

'See that tree?' Nkhandwe indicated a tall palm that stood a little way from the margin of the lake. 'If you will take me there, I will get it for you.'

'Very well,' said Ng'ona. 'Get on my back. The sooner I have your heart, the sooner my child will be cured.'

'The sooner we get there, the better,' agreed the little Jackal and he clambered on to the Crocodile's back. A fig came floating past and Nkhandwe picked it up and was about to eat it, when an idea flashed into his clever little mind. He thought he would hold on to the fig until he reached the shore. It might come in useful.

'Just put me down and I will run and get my heart for you,' said the Jackal, when they came to the sand,

and he popped the fig into his mouth and held it in the pouch of his cheek.

Ng'ona waited anxiously, while the Jackal ran to the palm tree and pretended to hunt for something hidden amongst its roots. Then he returned to the Crocodile, put his paw in his mouth and drew out a little purplish lump.

'There you are!' Nkhandwe cried, as he tossed the fig to Ng'ona. 'There is my heart! And much good may it do your child!'

'Thank you,' said the delighted Crocodile. 'I am very much obliged to you.' He picked up the fig, slid back into the water and swam away.

Nkhandwe gave a sigh of relief. What a silly Crocodile, he thought, but how fortunate that he should have been so silly! Then he began to laugh. He was still laughing when he saw the Crows go flying over to the island. This time they had no basket and the heartless little Jackal only laughed all the more!

THE INFALLIBLE SALT BIRD

'I'VE been robbed! Some scoundrel is stealing my salt and I demand that the thief be discovered!'

Fisi, the Hyaena, stamped on the ground in indignation and, with difficulty, Kalulu, the Rabbit, repressed a grin. Fisi was a most dishonest creature and it amused Kalulu to see the Hyaena making such a fuss now that he himself was the victim.

'Whom do you suspect?' asked Mkango, the Lion, to whose Court the Hyaena had brought his complaint.

'How should I know which rogue to suspect?' Angrily, he looked round the *bwalo* where all the animals were gathered and his eyes travelled slowly from Nyani, the

Baboon, to Khungubwe, the Crow; from Nkhandwe, the Jackal, to Vumbwe, the Civet; from Njusi, the Serval, to Kalulu, the Rabbit, and on the Rabbit they rested with the utmost malignancy.

'I suggest that you set a watch over your salt. Then, either it will not be stolen, or you will discover the thief.'

'I watched, myself, last night. Unfortunately, I fell asleep. . . .' A titter of laughter ran round the Court and Fisi turned and glared at the crowd. 'It is my belief,' he went on, 'that I was drugged. I found traces of a mysterious powder in my cave. The thief could have blown it there.'

'To be surc,' said the Lion, a little testily. 'You need to set a more cunning watch. Do not forget the saying that "where there are two, the thing will not be stolen". Next case!'

Before Fisi could protest at this summary dismissal of his complaint, there was a disturbance at the back of the Court. Someone was thrusting his way towards the centre of the *bwalo*. It was Mbanda, the Hyaena's cousin, and he was carrying a little goatskin bag.

'The stolen salt!' he cried, waving the *chibethi*, out of which a few white grains were falling from a hole in the side. 'I found it hidden at Kalulu's. . . .'

'What?' The Rabbit's exclamation was full of astonishment and a murmur of surprise came from the crowd.

'Why should you think that is the stolen salt?' Mkango asked, smoothly.

'I found a trail leading from my cousin's cave. A very faint trail, it was, but undoubtedly of salt. It led me to the big rock at Kalulu's home. And see!' Triumphantly, Mbanda indicated the hole in the goatskin bag. 'Here is the place from which the salt had fallen!'

A low growl came from Fisi, the Hyaena. He stood for a moment, scowling with fury, then turned and pointed a shaking paw at the Rabbit.

'Scoundrel! Robber!' he shouted. 'I name you as the thief!'

'Kalulu, the Rabbit, what have you to say to this accusation?' Mkango, the Lion, was now as interested as all the other animals. The case had taken a surprising turn, for no one would have suspected the Rabbit of stealing the Hyaena's salt.

All eyes were on Kalulu, as he stepped into the centre of the Court. He did not have a guilty air, but there was a look of wariness on his face.

'I know nothing of the Hyaena's salt,' he said, with a touch of hauteur.

'How, then, does it come to be hidden at your place?'

'Someone must have put it there without my knowledge,' the Rabbit replied.

'Do you recognize the goatskin bag?'

'Yes. The *chibethi* is mine, but I have not used it for a long time.'

'Ah!'

'Khungubwe, the Crow, was carrying a bag like that only the other day.' It was Nkhandwe, the Jackal, who offered this information.

'Lots of people have goatskin bags,' Khungubwe interposed hurriedly, but he looked decidedly uncomfortable and it was easy to guess that any bag he might possess was unlikely to have been come by honestly.

'Where is your *chibethi* now?' the Lion asked.

'I don't know. It has disappeared.'

'Is that it?' Mkango indicated the bag Mbanda held.

'Certainly not!' the Crow exclaimed, indignantly. 'My *chibethi* has no hole.'

'That proves nothing.'

'Two days ago, Nyani, the Baboon, was trading salt for pots of beer,' an aged Antbear wheezed.

'Indeed?' The Lion called Nyani. 'Where did you get the salt?' he demanded.

'I traded maize cobs for the salt,' the Baboon answered, sullenly.

'Ask him where he got the maize cobs!' suggested someone at the back of the crowd. Everyone laughed and the Antbear mumbled to his neighbour: 'Even if the salt was not stolen, I'll wager that the maize cobs were!'

'Silence!' roared the Lion. He turned to his advisers, who were busily conferring with each other. 'Have you anything you wish to say?' he asked.

'Yes.' It was the custom for a Judge to have three advisers, or Assessors, as they were called. On this occasion the three happened to be Katumbu, the Otter, Nungo, the Porcupine and Nadzikambe, the Chameleon. Katumbu was acting as their spokesman. 'We think that this inquiry will not lead us to the truth,' he said. 'Salt is precious. Salt is wealth and there are many rogues who might steal such a thing. We suggest that tonight, when the sun is down, each one of us shall have an opportunity to prove his innocence or guilt. Happily, when salt is stolen, there is an infallible way of discovering the thief.'

'Very well,' said the Lion. He seemed surprised at the Otter's words and, at once, everyone began to talk. Why 'when salt is stolen', they wondered? Several of the animals looked extremely glum and even the Hyaenas did not appear to be too pleased. What new magic was to be produced? What form would it take? Well, at one hour after sunset, they would know. . . .

The Lion gave an order and the Court was cleared. He then called the three Assessors to him. 'Tell me your plan,' he commanded. 'What is this infallible way? I have never heard of such a thing.'

'Have you not heard of the White Bird, the Guardian of all Salt?' Katumbu asked. Mkango shook his head. 'We will summon this bird tonight. Then, each one in his turn must lay his paws upon it and proclaim his innocence. If he is lying, the Salt Bird will know and, when all the animals have taken the oath, the bird will show us the thief.'

'Where is this fabulous bird to be found?' The Lion was greatly intrigued and full of curiosity.

'That is Nadzikambe's secret,' replied the Otter, and with that the Lion had to be content.

Kamba, the Tortoise, had slept late and, by the time he had finished his breakfast, the morning was well advanced. For all that, he thought he might as well stroll over to the Lion's *bwalo*, to listen to the latest gossip and find out what was going on.

He had not gone more than a few paces when he saw his friend Nadzikambe, the Chameleon, coming towards him.

'Kamba!' Nadzikambe called out urgently. 'I must talk to you. More salt has been stolen and I think our chance has come.'

'At last!' The Tortoise waited eagerly for the Chameleon to come up with him and, while they walked back together, Nadzikambe told him of the morning's happenings.

'Katumbu and Nungo thought the Salt Bird was a wonderful idea, so now we should be able to find out who it was that robbed you all those months ago.'

'With any luck!' Kamba agreed. He was more than a little excited, for he had waited a long time for just such an opportunity as this. Several months back, he had gone to market to exchange a load of vegetables for a bag of salt. On his way home, he'd been waylaid by two weird figures, wearing masks and long grass skirts. They had stunned him, flung him into a pit and made off with his bag of salt. He had no idea who the robbers could have been, but he had never given up hope of finding some clue to their identity. Meanwhile, he and Nadzikambe had evolved the idea of the Salt Bird, feeling sure it would prove effective, if only they could get a chance to put it to the test. Now, it seemed, the time had come.

'We must get the Salt Bird ready at once, while Katumbu is seeing to the preparations at the *bwalo*. Where are the materials?'

'Here,' said Kamba, uncovering a large basket in which lay a strange assortment of gourds, bamboo, grass and feathers, beeswax, berries, string. Lifting them out with care, the two friends set to work on the construction of the bird. Two gourds of different sizes made its head and body, two shining berries gave it bright and penetrating eyes. Its neck and legs were made of grass and reeds, the beak of yellow bamboo. This framework was then smeared with wax and covered with white feathers. It looked exactly like the pale ghost of some large Crane. The Chameleon and the Tortoise were delighted with the result. They stood back and surveyed their handiwork with pride, then, cunningly, they fixed a string or two to give the bird's head movement and mounted it upon a gourd the size of Kamba's shell.

'Now for the magic powder,' said Nadzikambe, and poured some white concoction over the white feathers.

'Of what did you make the magic powder?' Kamba asked with interest.

'Of little grains of truth,' the Chameleon answered, extravagantly. 'The secret of the powder must never be told or it will lose its power. Surely you know that?'

'Of course.' Kamba grinned at his friend. 'I was only thinking that I would have used a mixture of flour and finely powdered salt.'

'Perhaps I did,' the Chameleon grinned back. 'Who knows?'

While the preparations for the evening's ceremony were being made, a great deal of anxious speculation was taking place, especially amongst the animals whose consciences were far from clear. If only they knew what to expect! Could whatever-it-was detect *any* thief or only someone who had stolen salt? Khungubwe, the Crow, was particularly worried, for he had stolen the *chibethi*, though not from the Rabbit. He had taken it from one of the huts in the village and in it he had found a few grains of salt. Nyani, the Baboon, had stolen salt, but not from the Hyaena. The Hyaenas, themselves, were worried for, in their time, they had stolen many things, including salt, and Mbanda seemed unduly fidgety and nervous until Fisi pointed out that they had nothing to fear, since it was he who had brought the case.

'Pity you chose today to bring it,' Mbanda grumbled. 'Those Assessors are all friends of the Rabbit's.'

'How was I to know who the Assessors were to be?' Fisi protested. 'That was just my bad luck.'

'Well, I don't like it. Can't we get the Lion to call the whole thing off?'

'No. It's too late. You know perfectly well that he wouldn't do that now. Besides,' the Hyaena paused and looked at his cousin, 'I mean to know who stole my salt. You say it is that insufferable Rabbit, and if he's not guilty, then I want to know who is. Don't you?'

'Er . . . yes, of course,' Mbanda agreed hurriedly. 'It's just that I don't want any unpleasantness.'

'Where there are thieves, there is bound to be unpleasantness,' said Fisi, sententiously.

'Well, you should know.' An ugly sneer showed for a moment on Mbanda's face, then he looked up at the sky. 'We'd better be moving,' he said. 'It won't do for us to be late and the sooner we know what is in store, the better. Come on!'

The sun went down. The Cicadas and Bullfrogs tuned up for their nightly chorus. One by one, the stars appeared and, one by one, the Fireflies flashed their tiny lamps in rivalry. At the Lion's *bwalo*, a great fire had been lit and, gradually, the animals assembled round it. A drum started to throb, but ceased abruptly when Mkango, the Lion, and the three Assessors took their place beneath an ancient fig tree. The chattering of the crowd died down as the Lion began to speak.

'You know that the Hyaena's salt has been stolen and that Kalulu, the Rabbit, has been named the thief. Since the Rabbit maintains that he is innocent, we will now summon the Salt Bird to tell us if he speaks the truth. If he does, then others must swear their innocence and the bird will show us the true thief.' Mkango made a signal to the drummer, stepped forward and threw a handful of salt on the fire. A blue flame shot up and Mkango called upon the Salt Bird to appear.

'The Salt Bird? What kind of bird is that?' A murmur of wonder ran through the crowd and all the animals craned their necks and peered into the shadows beyond the fig tree. Something was moving through the whispering grasses, a great white bird that glided forward silently until it stood beside the Lion, in a little hollow, its feet quite hidden amongst fallen leaves. The murmur turned to one of awe. This was something new and strange indeed!

Laying his forepaws on the bird's white body, the Lion spoke again.

'Bambo Mbalame! You, who are the Guardian of all Salt, we pray you, show us the thief!' Mkango then faced

the three Assessors and raised his right paw above his head. 'I swear that I am innocent of stealing salt,' he said in a loud, clear voice.

Seeing that the Lion's paw was white with the magic powder, Nadzikambe, the Chameleon, made an almost imperceptible signal and the Salt Bird's head nodded in stiff confirmation of the Lion's innocence. Kalulu, the Rabbit, was then called. He, too, placed his paws upon the bird, faced the Assessors and swore. His paw, too, was white and the Salt Bird nodded again. Clearly, the Rabbit was not guilty, though Fisi, the Hyaena, could be heard to mutter: 'I don't believe it! I don't believe it!'

One after another, the animals came forward and took the oath. As the magic powder showed white on every paw, the atmosphere grew more and more tense. By the time that his turn came, Khungubwe, the Crow, was in a pitiable state of nerves and, just as he was about to lay a trembling claw upon the bird, an Owl chanced to hoot.

'Caw!' croaked Khungubwe, jumping straight up into the air. 'It wasn't me! It wasn't! I didn't steal the Hyaena's salt. I only took a *chibethi* from a hut. How was I to know that it had once held salt?'

'Return the *chibethi*!' The mysterious command seemed to come from the very ground on which the Salt Bird stood.

'Indeed I will,' said the Crow, thankful to have got off so lightly.

This exhibition of the Salt Bird's powers did nothing to bolster up the morale of Nyani, the Baboon. What, he asked himself, was the use of swearing he was innocent of stealing salt, when he wasn't? Wouldn't it be better to admit, right away, that he had taken some salt from the Chief's own store? Not the Hyaena's salt. Then, perhaps, he'd get off as lightly as Khungubwe?

Nyani was right and, when the mysterious voice ordered him to return as much salt as he had stolen, the Baboon congratulated himself on his sagacity in telling the truth. There were times, he decided, when it undoubtedly paid to do so.

By this time, the Hyaena was looking cross and disappointed, for only Vumbwe, the Civet, remained to take the oath. When he, too, proved guiltless of the theft, Fisi turned impatiently to the Lion. 'Someone stole my salt,' he grumbled. 'If it is not Kalulu, the Rabbit, then it must be one of the Assessors. They haven't taken the oath.'

'Nor have you, Fisi,' the Otter pointed out. 'Nor has your cousin, Mbanda.'

'We don't have to,' flared the Hyaena, indignantly. 'It was my salt that was stolen. . . .'

'Was it?'

Nobody was sure who had spoken and Fisi ignored the interruption. 'I can't steal from myself, can I?' he demanded, querulously.

'No. But your cousin could steal from you. Mbanda, lay your paws upon the Salt Bird and take the oath.'

It was an order that could not be disobeyed. Reluctantly, Mbanda shuffled forward, his mind whirling near the borderline of panic. One thought was uppermost: I must not be found out! If I put my paws on that bird, it will know that it was I who drugged my

cousin, took his salt and tried to incriminate that hateful Rabbit by stealing his *chibethi* and laying a trail to his home. I must not touch the bird . . . everything will be all right if I don't touch it . . . I'll just pretend to lay my paws upon it. . . .

A moment later, Mbanda raised his paw, on which no trace of magic powder showed. 'I swear that I am innocent of stealing s . . .' His voice faltered. Even before the Salt Bird cried 'You lie!' he could see from the look on the Assessors' faces that his guilt was obvious.

The Salt Bird whirled around and pointed at Mbanda with its beak. 'Here is your thief! Here is the one who stole the salt!' And it began to move towards the Hyaena.

'B-b-but how can my cousin be the thief?' stammered Fisi, momentarily bewildered by the discovery.

'I'm not, I'm not!' Mbanda tried to say, but no sound came, for the Salt Bird was belabouring him with its beak. 'Go away!' Mbanda yelled. 'Go away! How can you know I did it? I never touched you. Go away!'

'Because you dared not touch me, you gave yourself away,' the bird said, sternly. 'Assuredly, you are the thief!'

'What?' roared Fisi, scarcely able to believe his ears. 'It was you? My cousin? You stole my salt?'

'It was my salt as much as yours,' snarled Mbanda. 'You seem to have forgotten the day, some months ago, when we disguised ourselves in skirts and masks and stole

the bag from some poor, silly Tortoise. That was your idea and you persuaded me to help you and then refused to give me my share of the salt. You're mean, that's what you are! I saw no reason why I should not help myself to what was rightly mine. And if, at the same time, I could lay the blame on Kalulu, so much the better. You thought it was the Rabbit, didn't you? But for the Salt Bird . . .'

In sudden fury, Mbanda lashed out at the bird. For a moment it swayed perilously, then, in a cloud of white powder, it toppled over on its side. Beneath the gourd on which the bird was mounted, stood Kamba, the Tortoise. The Hyaenas gaped at him in horror, as he pointed an accusing paw at them.

'But for the Salt Bird,' he said, taking the words out of Mbanda's mouth, 'we might never have known who stole the salt or that it was the Hyaenas who took the bag, all that long time ago, from "some poor, silly Tortoise". The Salt Bird is indeed infallible!'

THE HUNTER'S CHILD

'Ai! Ai! Nyani! Baboons! The thieves are stealing our maize cobs! Come and chase them away!'

With shouts and cries the villagers ran to their gardens to pelt the abominable creatures with stones and drive them back to the thickly wooded mountain-side where they belonged.

'The Baboons are getting very bold and insolent!' remarked Tandaubwe, the Spider. He was busily repairing some minor damage to his web, while Nadzikambe lay sunning himself on the leaf of a gladiolus.

The Chameleon had been trying to compose a song, but the commotion in the village had upset his train of thought. 'You'd think they wouldn't dare to show their ugly faces here,' the Spider continued and spun another length of silver thread.

'It isn't so much their faces . . .' Nadzikambe grinned and left the sentence unfinished. A reminiscent look had come into his eye. 'The tale of the Hunter's Child and the Baboon has always been one of my favourites,' he said. 'Would you care to hear it?' he asked, hopefully.

'Just a moment while I finish this off.' Deftly, the Spider completed his work, then he moved closer to the Chameleon and settled down comfortably to listen. 'Well,' said Tandaubwe, 'what is the story?'

Nadzikambe cleared his throat. . . .

More than a hundred years ago, there lived a hunter. Herani was his name and he had an only child, a little boy called Achidu, and they lived all by themselves in a hut on the edge of the forest. The hut was full of treasures of the chase—ivory and skins and such—and thieves would sometimes plan to steal them. But the Hunter had a dog and his hut was strongly built and, as yet, no one had succeeded in breaking in. For all that, Herani always felt a little anxious if he had to leave the boy alone for any length of time; but someone had to stay and mind the chickens and it was not as if Achidu were a foolish, disobedient child. The little boy had plenty of sense.

'Now, remember,' Herani would say, as he sharpened his spear or tested a catapult, 'if you see anyone coming while I am away, shut yourself in the hut and do not open the door until you are absolutely certain that the visitor is a friend. I wish I could leave the dog with you, but I need him on this hunting expedition.' Then Herani would pick up his bow and arrows, give his son an affectionate cuff on the head and set off along the path that led to the forest with Garu, the Dog, trotting happily at his heels.

One day, when Herani had been gone for several hours, Achidu, who was collecting the hens' eggs, thought he saw something moving in the bushes beyond the Chickens' *khola*. Remembering his father's words, the small boy ran into the hut and bolted the door. The hut was round and had no window, so he could not see if anyone were approaching but, after a while, he heard the sound of flapping wings and a raucous croak: 'Caw! Caw! Caw!' Then there came a sharp tap on the door.

'Who knocks?' Achidu called out.

'A friend.'

'What friend? Tell me your name and why you are here?'

'I am Khungubwe, the Crow,' came the answer. 'I bring a message from your father.'

Achidu was instantly suspicious. Surely his father would never send a message by the Crow? Khungubwe did not rank as a friend.

'What is the message?' he asked, cautiously.

'Let me in and I will tell you,' said the Crow.

'If my father gave you a message, he must have told you that I would not open the door.' The little boy was very much on the alert. 'I cannot even be sure you are

Khungubwe. And you do not need an open door to give me a message!'

'Oh, yes, I do,' said the Crow, glibly. 'You see, I have a present for you. A present from your father,' he lied. 'As to my being Khungubwe . . . well, just a minute and I will give you one of my feathers. I'll push it under the door.'

There was a short pause, then, sure enough, a black feather—unmistakably a Crow's—was poked under the door. Achidu picked it up and examined it carefully, but he was thinking hard. Of course his father had not sent a present by a Crow! If he had a present, he would bring it himself when he came home. And, whether or no it really was Khungubwe outside, whoever it was was up to no good. Achidu was not to be fooled by any talk of presents!

'If you have a message for me, tell it,' he commanded. 'If you have a present for me, lay it on the ground and leave it there. My father told me not to open the door and I will not do so until he returns. It will not be long before he comes back.'

There was so long a pause after he had said this that he thought perhaps the Crow had gone away. But no. In a little while, Khungubwe was once more tapping on the door with his beak, *khu-khu-khu*, like a noisy Woodpecker. 'Your father isn't coming back today. That was the message,' said the Crow. 'So open the door, like a good boy, and let me give you the thing that he has sent.'

'I don't believe a word you say,' said Achidu. 'Please go away. Of course my father is coming back today.

Why . . .' Achidu had an inspiration and thought he'd try a piece of bluff. 'I do believe I see him coming in the distance now. Surely that is my father and our dog!'

'Caw!' squawked the Crow. He could see no sign of anyone himself, but he had no intention of risking an encounter either with Herani or his dog. As the Crow flew off, Achidu again heard the sound of flapping wings.

The little boy gave a sigh of relief. Then he grinned. He felt rather pleased with himself. The bluff seemed to have worked and now Khungubwe would think that he could see out of the hut. If only he could! Well, perhaps his father would make a spy-hole for him in the door? He would ask Herani as soon as he returned.

Meanwhile the Crow had flown straight back to the forest where Nyani, the Baboon, was anxiously awaiting his report.

'Ha! There you are at last!' exclaimed the Baboon, as Khungubwe landed on the branch of the tree against which he was lounging. 'How did it go? Have you made friends with the brat? Can we get into the hut?'

'No,' replied the Crow, shortly. 'The stupid boy wouldn't open the door—nasty, suspicious little wretch! He said he didn't believe me!'

The Baboon gave a snort of contempt. 'Huh! So you've bungled the job, have you? I might have known! I can't think why I ever sent you!'

'Bungled? Me? I bungled nothing!' The Crow protested indignantly. 'I did what you said. It was a bad plan to start with, that's what it was. You can't blame me if it didn't work. You've only got yourself to blame for that!'

'Oh, I blame myself all right!' The Baboon sounded as bitter as green casava. 'I blame myself for sending a blundering half-witted bird like you to do a job that any little Waxbill could have pulled off!'

Khungubwe's feathers fluffed up angrily. 'It's all very well for you to talk like that. . . .'

'You shut your silly beak!' snapped the Baboon rudely. 'To listen to you gives me a pain in my ears!'

'A pity it's not more general!'

Nyani glared at the Crow. 'Be quiet, I tell you!' he bawled. 'I want to think.'

'Caw!' croaked the Crow, with great contempt, and hopped on to another branch.

Silence reigned for a few minutes while Nyani alternately scratched his head or gnawed his nails. At length: 'Is there a window in the hut?' he asked. 'Can the brat see out?'

Khungubwe considered the question. 'There is no window, but the boy can see all right,' he replied.

'How d'you know that?'

'He said he thought he saw the Hunter and his dog in the distance. He wouldn't say that if he couldn't see, would he?' Khungubwe thought he had made a clever point.

'That could have been bluff,' Nyani sneered. 'Goodness knows, you are easy enough to fool! Did you see the Hunter yourself?'

'No. I didn't wait. I don't like that dog!'

'Well, I don't suppose the dog likes you, so that makes it even. Ha! ha! ha!' The Baboon treated himself to a loud guffaw.

'Caw!' croaked the Crow again. Nyani ignored him.

'We'd better assume that the brat can see, so that means some disguise.' Nyani was thinking aloud. 'Now, what shall it be? Some nice, friendly creature, I think, that could not possibly scare a little boy. . . .' He jumped up and started to pace up and down. 'I know!' he suddenly exclaimed. 'I've got it! Just the very thing!' He began to laugh. 'That old sheepskin of my grandfather's! If I take off my own fur coat, I can just get into it. And I make a beautiful sheep! Baa! Baa!' Nyani looked and sounded so comical that Khungubwe could not help laughing, too, and soon, their ill humour quite forgotten, the two thieves were busily working out the details of their plot.

Three days passed before they were able to put it into action. Herani, the Hunter, had again gone hunting. He had been exceedingly perturbed by his son's tale of the Crow, but had commended Achidu for his good sense, and he had made a cunning little spy-hole that he did not think anyone would notice from the outside of the hut. Then, as nothing untoward occurred during the next three days, he decided to set off once more with his dog. There was a Bush Turkey that he was particularly anxious to find. . . .

For an hour or so, Herani followed a twisting trail. The underbrush was thick, the trees tall and festooned with lianas and progress was slow, but the trail led to the more open country where the Bush Turkeys lived. He had almost reached it when Garu, the Dog, suddenly gave tongue and dived into a bush. A moment later he emerged with some furry object in his mouth, came bounding back and proudly laid the trophy at his master's feet. 'Just look what I have found!' was what he was clearly saying.

Herani looked. It was the skin of a Baboon, a very fine skin, golden-grey in colour and in perfect condition. How on earth, he wondered, had it come to be hidden away like that in a bush? It was very odd. Well, finding's keeping, he remembered, and he knew it was useless to continue with the hunt—Garu must have scared everything within miles—so Herani decided to return home. He wanted to 'treat' the skin right away. He'd go straight to the river near the hut and soak it, then peg it out in the sun to dry. From there, the dog could easily find his own way back to the hut and Achidu would then know that his father was not far away. What a delightful day it was, thought Herani, as he retraced his steps.

Achidu was sitting on the ground, sucking a stick of sugar cane, when he happened to look up and see a Crow flying towards the hut. Immediately he jumped up, slammed the door and bolted it. Then he put his eye to the new spy-hole. He found he could not see the Crow, but that was not surprising, for the spy-hole did not command a very wide view. Anyway, he thought, there was no reason why it should be Khungubwe. It could be just any Crow, flying from one place to another. . . .

A sudden commotion broke out in the Chickens' *khola*. Alarmed hens cackled frantically, squawks and screeches and cries of 'help-elp-elp-elp' rent the air and one frenzied hen could be heard protesting: 'He's stolen my egg, the lovely egg I laid this morning! Help-elp-elp-elp! Help!'

Achidu was trying to make up his mind as to whether or no he should go to their rescue, when another sound came to his ears—the bleating of a sheep.

'Baa! Baa!' The creature sounded distressed. 'Baa!' It butted its head against the door and spoke: 'Little boy! Let me in, let me in! There is a wicked Crow stealing your hens' eggs and I am afraid that it will come pecking at my eyes. Please open the door and save me from it!'

Again Achidu peeped through the spy-hole. An old, old sheep was standing at the door, such a harmless, foolish, odd-looking creature and it kept on bleating: 'Baa! baa! baa!' The little boy knew that he could not leave it to be pecked at by the Crow. He'd have to let it into the hut.

His hand was already on the bolt to draw it back, when yet another voice was added to the din—the voice of Garu, the Dog, barking his head off as he came racing up to the hut.

The Crow heard it and soared upwards. 'Caw! Caw!' he shrieked and flew away.

The Sheep heard it. 'My, oh, my!' it yelped, not sounding like a sheep at all, and took to its heels.

'Just let me catch you!' barked the Dog and gave chase.

Across the clearing they went, the Sheep moving as no sheep ever had or ever would, the Dog close behind him. It looked as if, in another minute, Garu must bring the creature down, but when it reached the first of the forest trees, it leapt up and swung itself into the branches. Utterly bewildered by this unexpected manœuvre—whoever heard of a sheep that could climb trees?—the

Dog stood barking at the foot of the tree. Slowly, his wagging tail drooped as it dawned on him that he had lost his quarry. It was a very dejected Garu that returned to Achidu for consolation.

After the hullabaloo at the Hunter's hut, the forest seemed very still and cool and peaceful to the Baboon. It had taken him some time to recover from that appalling chase. He had thought he'd never make the tree and he felt he'd hear that dog behind him for the rest of his days. The old sheepskin had not helped at all, when it came to running for dear life! Well, soon he'd be wearing his own comfortable skin again. Only a very short distance now to the bush where he had hidden it!

He was almost there when Khungubwe, the Crow, joined him.

'See what I mean about that dog?' Khungubwe began, hopping along beside the Baboon.

Nyani grunted. Suddenly he stooped down and examined the ground with care. Yes, it was the imprint of a man's foot that had caught his eye—a recent imprint—and here was the paw-mark of a dog! A horrid fear assailed him. He rushed to the hiding place and hurled himself at the bush.

'It's gone!' he screeched, a moment later. 'They've got my skin, I know it!' Nyani fairly danced with rage. 'My skin! We've got to find it! We've got to get it back! I can't be without a skin!'

'You've got that nice sheepskin,' Khungubwe pointed out. 'And you can't think how funny you look in it!' He started to laugh.

'Stop it!' screamed the Baboon. He picked up a stone, threw it at the Crow, then began to hunt through the bush all over again, but no skin was there. All he could find was a tuft of fur, dog's fur, the same colour as the hair of Garu's coat. He held it up.

'There!' he exclaimed. 'What did I tell you! It is that loathsome dog! How I hate the beast!'

'Well,' said Khungubwe, in a very bland voice, 'judging from the way the dog barked when you went up the tree, I'd say he hates you, too. And that,' he added maliciously, 'makes it quite even! Ha! ha! ha!'

There was a pause as Nadzikambe, the Chameleon, shifted his position. Tandaubwe, the Spider, was laughing heartily.

'Oh, don't stop,' he begged. 'I must know whether the Baboon did get his skin back.'

'Yes,' said the Chameleon. 'He found it next day, lying in the sun by the river, and managed to sneak off with it. But it no longer fitted him properly. You see, what with being soaked in the water and broiled in the sun, it had shrunk considerably, and Nyani had to cut a large hole near the base in order to be able to wear it. That is why the Baboons have no hair there—no hair at all.'

'Ah, yes, of course,' said the Spider. 'As the proverb says: "You can't skin a monkey's bottom!" I quite understand.'

THE CHAFERS AND THE DOVE

On a fallen tree near the river, six little Chafers sat watching the pageant of insects that winged their way to the pool from which the children of the Dragonfly were soon to emerge and come of age in all their iridescent beauty. With envious eyes, the Beetles gazed at the lovely creatures that flew by: Hornets, gaily striped in black and yellow, with gauzy wings that surely had been looted from the midnight sky; Butterflies with wings of velvet, blue as the turquoise, pale as opals; Butterflies in amber satin, gleaming like a golden sunset; Butterflies with gorgeous markings, all the colours of the rainbow. . . .

The little Chafers sighed. How wonderful to be beautiful, they thought, to be admired by everyone, invited everywhere. They were so drab that no one asked them anywhere at all.

'The wedding of the Red Dragonflies takes place in three days' time,' began Kamodzi, the eldest of the Beetles.

'And we shall not be invited to that, either,' said the second brother, Kawiri. He looked very down in the mouth.

'Unless we can find some way of making ourselves look gay and beautiful!'

All five Chafers turned to their youngest brother, Kamwana. 'How can we do that?' they asked. 'Have you any ideas?'

'Yes,' he answered brightly. 'There are flowers that are as gay as any Butterfly. Why shouldn't we make use of them?'

'How? In what way?'

'Could we not cover ourselves with the most brilliant petals, give ourselves new coats?'

'They'd never stay on,' objected Katatu, the third Beetle.

'They'd stay on if we used beeswax.' A note of enthusiasm had crept into the fifth Beetle's voice. Kasanu was beginning to think that there might be something in his brother's idea. So were the others. Eagerly, they discussed the possibilities. There was a shrub with vivid purple flowers, now in full bloom on the hillside. That, they thought, would make them look as royal as any Chief. Or there was the disa, bluer than the bluest sky, but perhaps its petals were too small?

'Glossy green leaves would make good, strong coats,' Kawiri ventured. He had a practical turn of mind.

'Spots are considered handsome,' murmured the fourth Beetle, Kanai, who admired them very much himself. 'There are plenty of flowers with spots.'

'We could all have different coats,' Kasanu suggested.

'Oh, I don't think that would do. We are brothers. We should look alike.' The eldest Chafer did not approve of any form of departure from family tradition.

'Then let's be purple,' they all chorused. 'We'll look fine in purple!'

'Very well, then,' said Kamodzi, 'purple it shall be. Now, don't let us waste any time. The first thing to get is some beeswax, then we must find the purple shrub. Let us go at once to the Bees.'

'Yes, let's.'

The six Beetles clambered down from their tree-trunk and scuttled off to the nearest hive. They had no difficulty in persuading the Bees to let them have some wax—the Bees were always willing to oblige their neighbours—but it took them much longer to find the purple shrub than they had expected. The first bush the Chafers came to had had its blossoms battered by a recent storm, the next was still in bud. So on they plodded, regardless of the mud, the thorny scrub, the long wet grass, until at last they came upon a bush whose flowers were newly opened and had all the qualities that they had hoped to find. The petals were a glossy purple and just the size to make a Beetle's coat.

'What could be better?' they asked, delightedly, and climbed up the shrub and began to bite through the stems of the finest sprays of blossom. When they had gathered enough, the Chafers clambered down again, formed a circle and carefully smeared each other's backs with wax. Then they took the purple petals and pressed them on.

'Now, how do we look?' The Beetles stood back to survey the result of their labours.

It certainly was colourful, but not as smart as they had hoped. A little of the mud from their feet seemed to have stained the coats and the purple petals were fast losing their sheen. In fact, the effect was rapidly becoming tatty and the Beetles had to admit that the experiment was not a success. They could no more hope to go to a wedding clothed in tatty purple than they could in their original drab coats.

'The colour is nice,' Kasanu said, but there was no mistaking the disappointment in his voice, or the doleful tones in which his brothers agreed that the colour was, indeed, very pleasing.

'But the coats won't do!' Reluctantly, Kamodzi made his pronouncement and the other five Beetles nodded their heads. They all looked very depressed and nobody spoke for several minutes. Then Kawiri returned to his original suggestion about leaves.

'Glossy green leaves would be all right, I am sure. They'd be much stronger and we could wash off any stains. What's more, we could use gum from the acacia tree for sticking. That would be better than wax.'

'Less messy, perhaps?'

'What do you think?'

'It's worth trying!'

'We'd look fine in shiny green!'

'Very well,' said Kamodzi. 'Shiny green we'll be! Let us collect some gum, then find the strongest, glossiest, greenest leaves we can.'

Off they set again, plodding through the mud, the thorny scrub, the long wet grass, until they had gathered all the materials they needed for their new green coats. Then, as before, they formed a circle, smeared each other's backs with gum and pressed the leaves in place. Where the covering was too large, they nibbled away at the leaf until the coats were a perfect fit. Then, once again, they stood back to survey the result of their labours.

It was not at all bad! The coats looked a little clumsy, perhaps, but the colour was good and the sheen was truly handsome. The Beetles walked all round each other, making little sounds of admiration, then they turned to their eldest brother. 'What do you think? Will the coats do?' They waited anxiously for his opinion.

'Y-yes, I think they will,' Kamodzi said slowly. 'I think the coats look very nice indeed.'

'Ai! Ai! Ai!' Rubbing their legs against their bodies, the little Beetles produced shrill stridulations of delight and they began to dance with pleasure. 'We have green coats!' they sang, as they stamped their feet.

Ai! Ai! Ai!
We have green coats,
  green coats!
We have new coats,
  new coats!
In our coats
  we'll go,
We'll go
  to a wedding!

They danced and sang until they were quite exhausted, so exhausted that they crawled under the nearest log of wood and fell fast asleep.

During the night it rained, but when morning came the sun shone brightly, between showers, and made the grasses look as if their heads had bent beneath a weight of diamonds. The Chafers woke, stretched their hairy legs and crawled out into the shining world. They blinked a little, remembered their new coats and turned to admire each other. . . .

'Ooh!' A long-drawn wail of disappointment greeted the discovery that their coats had lost their gloss and were rapidly turning brown. Already, they looked almost as drab as they had always done.

'It's no good,' the Beetles sighed. 'We are not meant to be beautiful!' Miserably, they sat down and tried to clean themselves up a bit. A Squirrel ran past. 'Well!' he called out. 'You are a dismal-looking lot, to be sure! What's the trouble?' He halted for a moment to look more closely at the Beetles.

'We want to have gay coats,' the eldest Chafer explained. 'We've tried making them from flowers and leaves, but it doesn't work. The colour fades.'

'Oh, well,' said the Squirrel, 'there's only one thing for you to do!'

'What's that?' the Beetles chorused, eagerly.

'Fly through a rainbow! At least, that's what Nkhunda, the Dove, says. Good luck to you!' The Squirrel laughed and continued on his way.

'Fly through a rainbow? Do you think he really means that?'

A buzz of discussion followed.

'It's all very well to say "fly through a rainbow", but there's got to be a rainbow first!'

'That's true.'

'It is the weather for rainbows.'

'Let's try it,' urged Kamwana.

'But we fly so clumsily!'

'Yes. We always fall on our backs, and then there's that awful struggle to get right way up again. I don't like flying.'

'Oh, do let's try it,' Kamwana pleaded once again.

'By all means,' Kamodzi agreed, 'if we see a rainbow.'

Immediately, the little Beetles looked upwards. The sun still shone and rain clouds were chasing one another across the sky. At any moment Chiuta, the God of Space, might place his bow in the heavens. The Beetles waited, hopefully, as a thin rain began to fall. Minutes passed . . . an hour passed . . . at last the lovely bow appeared, a glorious arc of colour that stretched across the sky and rested—where? Somewhere in the trees on the far side of the river, or so it seemed. The Chafers started to run towards it, but when they reached the river bank, they halted. How were they to cross the river? To attempt to fly would surely be too great a risk, for the river was wide and the current strong and one or other of the Chafers would be certain to fall in and get drowned. If only they could find someone to ferry them over! An obliging Crocodile, perhaps? But the river bank appeared to be deserted. The Beetles stood looking despondently around, fearing the rainbow would vanish before they could reach it.

'Couldn't we make a raft?' Katatu suggested, not very optimistically.

'I don't think that would be at all safe!' Kanai had always been more timid than his brothers. 'Anyway, it would take too long. By the time it was ready, there'd be no rainbow to fly through!'

'Why should you want to fly through the rainbow?' asked a gentle voice. The little Chafers hurriedly turned round and saw a grey bird standing quietly behind them. It was Nkhunda, the Dove, and she was looking at them with considerable interest. She repeated her question. 'Tell me why you want to fly through the rainbow?'

'We want to be beautiful,' said the Beetles, simply, and Nkhunda listened with sympathy while they told her their story. When they had finished, the Dove smiled at them. 'Climb on my back,' she said, 'and I will fly you through the rainbow. Then, if there is beauty in you, you will look beautiful.'

'Nkhunda! Will you really take us? How kind you are!' The little Chafers could scarcely believe their luck and scrambled on to the Dove as fast as they could. Settling themselves at the back of her neck, just clear of her wings, they looked like some strange collar or half a string of beads. A thrill of excitement welled up inside them as the Dove rose into the air. In a few moments, they were safely over the river . . . now the rainbow seemed quite close . . . closer . . . closer, its colours growing brighter every minute. . . .

The little Chafers never knew exactly when they passed through the arc. One moment, the rainbow was in front and they were brown and drab; the next, it was behind and they . . . what had happened to them? Had they become beautiful? They scarcely dared to look. Slowly, slowly they turned their heads. There seemed to be a radiance all around them and they, themselves, were now a shining green—a glorious metallic green that still held all the colours of the rainbow. A little sigh of happiness escaped the Beetles and the Dove flew back to earth. 'Now let me look at you,' she said.

With beaming faces, the Chafers climbed down and stood before Nkhunda.

'Yes, oh, yes!' Nkhunda said, with pleasure. 'Now you are beautiful indeed!'

The delighted Chafers immediately began to dance and sing.

Ai! Ai! Ai!
We have green coats,
rainbow coats!
We have new coats. . . .

The song died abruptly. The smiles faded from the Chafers' faces to be replaced by looks of consternation. In a horrified silence, they pointed at Nkhunda's neck. Her plumage was still grey, but where the Beetles had clung, their feet had left a dark, dark stain, a band of blackish brown.

'Look!' they wailed. 'Oh, look at the dreadful mark we've made! We forgot to clean our muddy feet! Nkhunda, will it ever come off?'

The Dove shook her head. 'Not if the rainbow has fixed it there,' she replied, and turned her neck to see what sort of mark it was. It looked to her like a handsome dark collar and she smiled with relief. Collars were a sign of rank and by no means to be despised! 'There is nothing to worry about,' she reassured the Beetles and, at that moment, a pair of Dragonflies—Red Dragonflies—came whirling by. Seeing the Dove's collar, they dipped their wings in respectful greeting, then the Chafers' gleaming coats caught their eye. The Dragonflies flew on a little way, whispering: 'Did you see?'

'Those glorious green creatures?' one muttered. 'Who could they have been?'

'They looked a little like the Chafers,' the other said, 'but such noble Chafers! Never have I seen such a wonderful green. They could not look more beautiful if their coats had been fashioned from the rainbow! Let us make sure that they are coming to the wedding with all our other fine insect guests.'

The Red Dragonflies turned back and flew up to the Beetles.

'*Tikuona!* We see you!' they said, with great respect. 'You will, we hope, honour us with your presence at our brother's wedding?'

Scarcely able to conceal their delight, the little Chafers bowed politely.

'*Zikomo*. We thank you,' they replied. 'It will indeed be a pleasure!' With difficulty, they managed to restrain themselves until the Dragonflies had gone away. Then, once more, they broke into a wild dance of joy. Round and round the Dove they circled, cheering, stamping, singing:

Ai! Ai! Ai!
Nkhunda is our friend!

Nkhunda wears a collar,
Nkhunda wears a ring,

Nkhunda is the Ring Dove,
Nkhunda is our friend!
And we are wearing
green coats,
new coats,
rainbow coats!
In our coats
we are going
To a wedding feast!
A wedding feast!
A wedding feast!
Nkhunda is our friend!

THE FEAST OF PLUMS

Ripe
Red
Plums!
Ripe
Red
Plums!

There'll be
A luscious
Feast
When
Summer
Comes!

Green
Plums
Will mellow
And
Ripen
In the Sun.

Soon,
There'll be
Ripe
Red
Plums
For everyone!

NADZIKAMBE, the Chameleon, laughed as he finished his song and turned to Guapi, the Duiker. 'What a party we'll have,' he said. 'I must compose a special song for the occasion. How soon do you think the plums will be ready?'

With his head on one side, the Duiker considered the little green fruits. They were fat and round and fully grown, but still hard and sour, and they needed a week of sunshine before they would be sweet and red and juicy. By the time the moon was new, Guapi decided, the plums should be reaching perfection.

'I think,' he said slowly, 'that it would be safe to hold the feast when the next moon is old enough to show in the night sky.'

Nadzikambe nodded his head in agreement. 'Just what I was thinking,' he drawled. 'Now, whom shall we ask to the party? Tortoise and Lemur, of course, and your Antelope cousins. What about Nkhandwe, the Jackal?'

'Yes. I think we ought to have Nkhandwe. He loves plums.'

'So does Vumbwe, the Civet, but I hope you'll have more sense than to invite him! He is ill-mannered and greedy and no friend of yours.'

'I know. We'll draw the line at Vumbwe.'

'Huh! You will, will you!'

The harsh and unexpected voice made Guapi jump, and the Chameleon hurriedly swivelled his eyes around in search of the speaker. It had sounded like Vumbwe himself, yet surely it could not be he? The Civet had never been seen abroad in daylight.

'Who's that?' Guapi demanded, but the only answer was a rasping snarl and something shot through the underbrush and vanished into the dark of the forest.

The Chameleon and the Duiker stared after it for a moment, then turned and looked at each other with questioning eyes.

'Could that have been Vumbwe, do you think?' Guapi whispered.

The Chameleon shook his head. 'No. He's *never* out before dark. All the same . . .' Nadzikambe paused and stared into the depths of the forest. '. . . it did sound like Vumbwe,' he admitted with a puzzled frown.

'Oh, dear! I wonder how much he overheard?'

'Next to nothing, I should say. But it can't have been the Civet—just one of those Weasely creatures, I expect: they are always sticking their noses into everything! Anyway, it is no good worrying.' The Chameleon refused to be upset by the incident. 'Let's get back to our plans for the party,' he said cheerfully. 'We must have Mole, mustn't we?'

'Yes.'

'And Otter and Frog?'

'Yes.' With an effort, Guapi dragged his mind away from the mysterious snarling stranger, who was soon forgotten by the two friends as they compiled their list of guests. So absorbed were they in their task that it was dark by the time that they had finished. Nadzikambe, very sensibly, made up his mind to spend the night where he was and Guapi decided to go down to the river. He knew that he'd find most of his friends at the drinking pool and he wanted to tell them about the party.

Bidding the Chameleon a very good night, Guapi skipped into the long grass and hastened away. As he trotted along, a gay little sound tinkled on tu the night wind and the Duiker smiled. He had no difficulty in recognizing the thin notes of the Chameleon's *bangwe*. A moment later, Nadzikambe's voice could be heard. 'Ripe red plums,' he was singing:

Ripe
Red
Plums!
Ripe
Red
Plums!

Oh, what
A feast
We'll have
Of ripe
Red
Plums!

In his lair at the edge of the forest, Vumbwe, the Civet, sat gnawing his claws. That evening, for the first time in his life, he had set out for the drinking pool before it was dark and on the way he had heard a strange voice singing a song about plums—his favourite fruit. Peering through the bushes, he had seen a Duiker, but he had not been able to identify the singer. Then a conversation had ensued and he had heard his own name. At the recollection, Vumbwe bristled with rage. How dare they call him greedy and ill-mannered! How dare they plan to hold a feast without him! A feast of plums, at that! They drew the line at *him*, did they? All right, then! If *he* was not to be asked, he'd spoil their feast for them! He'd get ahead of them somehow and eat their luscious plums. He'd make them look silly—feel silly, too!

Yes, but how?

(*Gnaw, gnaw, gnaw.*)

Supposing he were to walk into the party and scare the life out of them all? (*Gnaw, gnaw.*) But they mightn't be scared . . . and there might be someone bigger and stronger than himself amongst the guests . . . so that wouldn't do. Very well, then, supposing he were to disguise himself? Yes, but as what? As a Lion? No, he wasn't big enough. As a Python? No, he wasn't that sort of shape. As . . . as a . . . oh, but of course! What a wonderful idea!

Vumbwe jumped up excitedly. Of course that was the right disguise, he sniggered. He'd just got to get hold of it, that was all. He could steal it from the Hunter's hut in the village over the hill. It meant a little careful planning, but to a clever Civet, like himself, that was nothing!

Pacing up and down, his mean face puckered in thought, Vumbwe began to work out the details of his scheme. First, there was the theft of the disguise. He'd have to wait near the village and lie low until the Hunter went off on an expedition, then he could sneak into the hut and take what he wanted from amongst the many trophies of the chase that must be stored there. Next, he would have to deal with the Duiker . . . he'd need rope for that—plenty of rope, good, strong vine-rope from the thickest part of the forest—he could lay in a stock of that right away. . . .

Smirking with pleasure at the way his plot was taking shape and with the vision of a hundred ripe red plums to goad him on, Vumbwe, the Civet, set off for the place where the finest lianas grew.

Nadzikambe, the Chameleon, was puzzled. He had not seen his friend, Guapi, for several days and now the night of the feast had come. At any moment the guests would be arriving and there was no sign of the Duiker. It really was very worrying and so unlike Guapi to be late, so unlike him not to have sent a message. The Chameleon could not understand it at all. True, rumour said that the Duiker had been ill—nothing serious, just a cold or a sore throat or something affecting his voice—and he'd thought it wise to lie up so as to make sure of being fit for the party, but Nadzikambe knew that rumour could not be trusted and he would have liked a definite assurance that all was well. He had made what preparations he could for the feast. All the invitations had been given and accepted. The plums had been gathered and stacked in crimson mounds beneath the tree, where they now gleamed like heaps of jewels in the pale moonlight. A broken *bangwe* string had been replaced and a new song composed for the occasion. There was nothing more, Nadzikambe felt, that he could do.

He picked up the instrument and strummed for a few moments in a half-hearted fashion. A rustle in the long grass made him stop abruptly . . . perhaps this was Guapi at last? He peered round, hopefully . . . but no, it was the first of the guests—Nkhandwe, the Jackal.

With him were Kamba, the Tortoise, and Zonde, the Frog.

The Chameleon greeted them effusively, then apologized for the Duiker's absence and asked if, by any chance, they had news of him. 'I can't understand what has happened,' he said. 'It is so unlike him to have sent no message.'

'Perhaps he has been delayed,' the Jackal suggested. 'I hear there has been trouble in the village over the hill. Something has been stolen and they say that the Hunter and his friends are out searching for the thief. Maybe Guapi has had to make a detour to avoid them.'

'Well, that may easily be the case.' Nadzikambe sounded relieved. 'I've heard nothing of this. Tell me, what has been stolen, and do they know who the thief is?'

'I don't know,' replied the Jackal. 'My guess is Nyani, the Baboon.'

'It can't have been Nyani. He and Bushpig have been away on a raid.' This information was volunteered by Changa, the Lemur, who had just arrived, whereupon speculation as to whom the thief might be became general, while the Chameleon moved slowly round, welcoming the other guests who had assembled. Questions and answers hovered in the air like a cloud of moths.

'Who could the thief have been?'

'Fisi, the Hyaena, perhaps.'

'What was it that was stolen?'

'A skin and a pair of horns.'

'Whatever for?'

'Who could want to steal those?'

'I can't imagine,' said a strange, husky voice, and everyone turned to look at the newcomer. A joyous shout greeted him: 'Guapi! Here you are, at last! What happened?'

'I had to go a long way round,' the newcomer answered. His voice sounded extraordinarily hoarse and odd. 'The forest is full of villagers armed with sticks and spears. I didn't want to be seen by them.'

'Of course not. They were looking for a thief,' Changa explained. 'I expect you know all about the robbery at the village?'

'What do you mean? Why should I?' The Duiker spoke brusquely and Nadzikambe looked at him in surprise. He'd never heard Guapi speak like that before and really his voice was very peculiar. He even looked a little peculiar—his eyes seemed smaller and lighter in colour and his legs less slender. A trick of the light, Nadzikambe supposed and, of course, the Duiker had been ill. People with colds and sore throats often looked and sounded a bit queer. He thought no more about it and tried to catch the Duiker's eye. 'Oughtn't we to start on the plums?' he mouthed.

The Duiker nodded. 'Come on, everybody!' he called out, still in that odd, husky voice. 'This is a Feast of Plums and I mean it to be a proper feast. Each go and choose yourself a fine plum and then I will make sure that you have chosen well.' He bustled round and waved the animals towards the heaps of fruit. Each guest then selected the plum he most fancied but, before he could eat it, the Duiker took it from him and sampled it himself. 'Oh, my dear Kamba!' he would exclaim, or

'My dear Nkhandwe! This one isn't good enough for you. You must find yourself a better plum than this!' And when the 'better plum' had been selected, he'd sample that and, with his jaws dripping juice, he'd say: 'Mmm! Tha'sh not sho bad, but YOU should only eat the finesh plums. Nothing but the best is goo' 'nough for YOU! Do look for a *really* good one!' In this way he succeeded in eating all the best plums himself and the guests scarcely got any.

Nadzikambe watched this extraordinary behaviour with growing concern. He simply could not believe his eyes. That Guapi, of all people, should act so strangely! It was incredible! The guests, too, were more than a little surprised and were beginning to look at each other and to mutter under their breath: 'What's the matter with Guapi?' and 'It's all very well to be a good host, but isn't he rather overdoing it?' And a few were saying: 'That was a lovely plum I'd chosen and he's eaten it himself. That's not good manners!' Nadzikambe did not know what to do. Dare he say anything to the Duiker? If he didn't, he felt, the party would be an utter failure and Guapi would never live down the disgrace . . . and he himself would be blamed to a certain extent. He'd have to say something, he decided, and waited until the Duiker came close, then plucked at his foreleg to attract attention. 'I say,' he began, in a low voice.

'Don't lay your sticky hands on me!' the Duiker snarled.

The Chameleon shrank back amazed, his brain in a whirl. Where had he heard that snarl before? No Duiker ever snarled like that! But he knew that snarl, had heard it recently . . . but where? WHERE? Ah! He'd been talking to Guapi and someone had spoken and snarled and vanished into the bush . . . someone who had overheard their plans . . . someone who might have been Vumbwe, the Civet. That was it. What, then, had happened? The Chameleon turned over every possibility in his mind. Could Vumbwe have laid a spell on Guapi to make him behave in this strange way? It didn't seem likely. Could the Duiker be an imposter—Vumbwe, himself, disguised? That seemed more probable, but where could he have got the disguise? That skin and those horns? And what had happened to Guapi? What indeed? It did not bear thinking about . . . or didn't it? A skin and some horns had been stolen from the Hunter's hut. Could it have been a Duiker's skin? A pair of Duiker horns? Could Vumbwe, the Civet, have been the thief?

A flurry of earth behind him interrupted Nadzikambe's train of thought and he turned to see Mfuko, the Mole, cautiously emerging from the ground.

'Mfuko!' the Chameleon said in an urgent whisper, 'Stay where you are. I must speak to you.'

'I've so much to tell you,' answered an equally urgent and breathless small voice, 'about Guapi, the Duiker. . . .' Mfuko remained half in, half out of his tunnel.

'Yes?'

'Vumbwe, the Civet, laid a trap for him some days ago. Guapi was caught and has been kept a prisoner ever since. The Hunter found him—bound to a tree near Vumbwe's lair. When he heard Guapi's story, he set him free and now they are searching for the Civet.'

'The Civet is here—I am sure of it—disguised as

Guapi. He took us all in,' Nadzikambe explained, 'but his behaviour was so strange that I began to wonder, and when he snarled at me and spoke, he gave himself away. What are we to do?'

'I think Guapi is on his way here. He has some sort of plan, so let us join the party and pretend that nothing is wrong.'

Together, the Mole and the Chameleon moved towards the dwindling heaps of plums. As they reached them, an unearthly wail rose on the air and, in the startled silence that followed, a deep voice spoke from somewhere close at hand.

'Beware! Beware!' it said. 'All you who feast, beware! One of your number is a thief and an imposter! Mlungu, the Great Spirit, has sent his Messenger to show him to you!' Then, from the long grass, stepped the weirdest creature. It wore a mask and head-dress made of grass and bark, a skirt of grass, such as a dancer might affect, and, on a wooden platter, it carried a mysterious ball. Speechless with awe and amazement, the animals stood and watched this Messenger walk straight up to their host and offer him the ball.

The Duiker stared at it and began to tremble, then: 'Go away!' he shouted. 'I don't want your ball. This is a trick! Go away!' And everyone noticed that his voice was no longer husky but loud and shrill, like the voice of the Civet.

'The ball is for you,' the Messenger said. 'You are the host, are you not? The ball will show you the imposter. Take it. It is your duty to your guests!' He held the platter towards the Duiker.

'I don't want it. Take the hateful thing away!' the Duiker screeched and lashed out with his foreleg, and because the ball was made of beeswax, it stuck to his leg. In a frenzy he danced about, trying to extricate himself and, when he could not do so, he foolishly attempted to kick the ball away, so that another leg got stuck. In vain he raged and roared and, after a few more frantic efforts to get free, he fell down and lay on the ground with all his legs stuck fast together.

'There's the imposter! There's the thief!' the Messenger called out and flung off his own disguise. 'See! I am Guapi!' he cried, 'and this, if I am not mistaken, is Vumbwe, the Civet. What shall we do with him?'

'Strip him of his coat and horns!'

'Treat him like the thief he is!'

'Plaster him with wax and stick the plum-stones on him. That's the way to treat a thief!'

'Yes! Yes! He's eaten all the best plums. Now he can have the stones as well!'

With that, they set upon the Civet, ripped off the stolen Duiker skin and smeared him with beeswax. Then, amidst much laughter, they peppered him with plum-stones and soon he was quite unrecognizable and looked a very comical creature indeed.

'Now, off you go,' they said, 'and think yourself lucky for, if you meet the Hunter, you will be safe. He won't know who you are and, if we give him back the things you stole, maybe he will be satisfied.'

Vumbwe, the Civet, waited for no second bidding, but ran from the place just as fast as his sticky legs would permit, while the rest of the party gaily settled down to finish off the few remaining plums. When they were done, Nadzikambe reached for his *bangwe.*

'*Olé! Olé!*' he sang, and played a chord. 'I had composed a Song of Plums for this occasion, but another song has just come to me which I will sing instead. It is a thoughtful song.

Olé! Olé!
The loud voice
betrays the Civet,
The grunt
betrays the Hog.
Spots betray
the lissom Leopard,
The bark
betrays the Dog.

There's a moral
to these sayings,
And you
will agree,
We all have something
that betrays us—
Even you,
and even me!

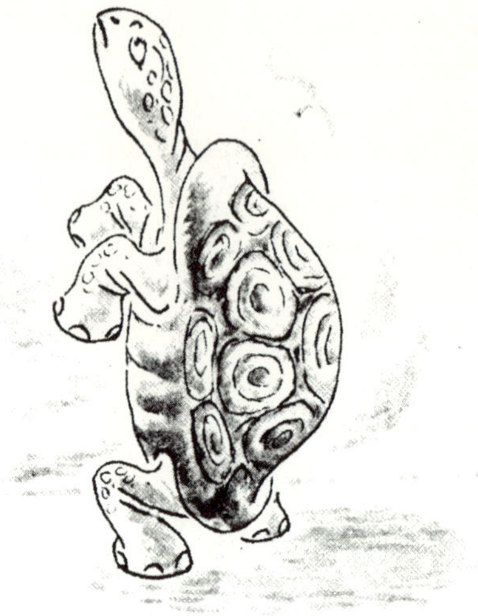

THE MAGIC BONE

'ALL this dust!' grumbled Kamba, the Tortoise, as the thin grey spiral of a dust-devil whirled past and went dancing away over the sun-baked land. 'It is high time that the rains came. They've never been so late before.' He coughed and looked up at the cloudless sky. 'Not a sign,' he muttered. 'Not a sign!'

'Mph!' snorted Nadzikambe, the Chameleon. 'The only rain we'd get in this weather is monkeys' rain!'

'Monkeys' rain?' queried the Tortoise. 'What do you mean?'

Nadzikambe smiled. 'It's an old story,' he said. 'It all happened a long, long time ago. Like now, there had been a drought. . . .'

There had been a drought and food was very scarce. All the animals were getting thinner and thinner and more and more anxious. All, that is, save one. Mkango, the Lion, alone looked sleek and fat. And the strange thing was that Mkango had almost given up hunting and now only left his cave at sunset to go down to the river for a drink. Each evening he would stalk majestically to the water, ignoring everyone he met except the Rhinoceros, with whom he would sometimes exchange a few words or pause for a moment's gossip. Then, back he would go to his cave. It was all very peculiar.

'How is it that Mkango is so fat?' the animals asked each other. 'What does he eat? Where does he get his food?'

'He must have a secret store in his cave,' someone suggested.

'If he has, he's mean not to give us anything.'

'Well, he is mean. We all know that!'

'He certainly is,' agreed Tandaubwe, the Spider, 'but . . .' he paused and drew a deep breath. 'I know his secret!' he announced pompously.

'You do?'

'Yes,' said the Spider. 'I may say that I, too, have been wondering about Mkango and his food—I am always interested in food. . . .'

'Yes, we all know that!' murmured Kalulu, the Rabbit.

'So, yesterday, I decided to visit his cave. . . .'

'You did?' The animals crowded excitedly round the Spider. 'What happened?' they asked eagerly.

'Of course, Mkango had no idea that I was there. He never saw me at all. Dear me, no! He was far too intent on his cooking!' Again Tandaubwe paused for effect.

'Cooking? Mkango? What was he cooking?'

'A bean. One little brown bean.'

'Go on. What else?'

'A bone.'

'What sort of bone?' Kalulu demanded. 'A big, juicy bone with plenty of meat?'

'No.' The Spider shook his head. 'It was a little, little bone with no meat at all. And that was all that he put into his cooking pot.'

'One bean and a little meatless bone?' Mystified, astonished, puzzled, the animals looked at each other, then back at Tandaubwe. 'What sort of sense does that make?' they asked.

'Plenty of sense, apparently,' said the Spider, 'for the bone has great magic, so it seems.'

'Ah!' The animals were relieved. A magic bone was something they could understand. 'What is its magic? How does it work?'

'Very simply indeed. It just fills the pot with whatever it is placed beside,' Tandaubwe explained. 'In no time at all, the Lion's pot was full of beans. All he had to do was add a little water and cook them over his fire. Now you know why Mkango is sleek and fat. He has all the food he wants!'

'And he never gives anything away, never invites

anyone to his cave!' The animals clicked their tongues and shook their heads in disapproval. Such meanness, they felt, was unforgivable. Mkango should be ashamed of himself!

'The Lion has a magic bone that fills his pots with food!'

Like a summer hatch of Butterflies, the news spread through the district until it reached the Mole in his underground home, the Eagle in his mountain aerie, even the little Monkeys who lived in the tops of the tallest trees.

'A magic bone that fills the food pots? That is exactly what we need!' A little grey Monkey sighed wistfully. 'How else can we provide a wedding feast for our daughter?'

How else indeed? As the day of the wedding drew nearer and nearer, this problem had perplexed the Monkeys more and more. Soon the bridegroom, his friends and his relations, would be arriving, and what had they to offer them? A few nuts. A dozen wizened berries. A handful of beans. Barely enough to keep them alive, and there was nothing for the other wedding guests. What were they to do, the Monkeys wondered for the hundredth time. What could they do?

'If only we could borrow the Lion's magic bone,' said Nthanda, the mother of the bride-to-be.

'Why not? That would solve the problem entirely!' Nyonyo, the father, clapped his hands excitedly. 'Surely Mkango would not refuse to lend it for a wedding feast? No one could be so mean!'

'At least we can ask. No harm in asking.'

'We must send a messenger at once. There is no time to lose.' A shrill chattering broke out as all the members of the family offered their suggestions as to whom the messenger should be. Nkhandwe, the Jackal? Kalulu, the Rabbit? Someone large and important like Njobvu, the Elephant?

'Not Njobvu,' Nyonyo decided. 'He is so disobliging. And Nkhandwe is not very reliable. But Kalulu, the Rabbit, is helpful and clever. We will ask him to act for us. Nthanda and I will go and see him right away.' The little grey Monkeys leapt up, sprang gracefully from branch to branch and went swinging through the tree-tops at a great pace.

Within an hour, they had found Kalulu and had told him their troubles and, full of sympathy, the Rabbit said that he would be delighted to be their go-between and carry their request to the Lion. So that evening, when Mkango emerged from his cave, much to his surprise, he found a deputation waiting for him. The Rabbit greeted him with great politeness and, when the customary civilities had been observed—with noticeable reluctance on the Lion's part—Kalulu came to the point. Was not Mkango the fortunate possessor of a magic bone? It was the envy of all the animals.

The Lion at once looked wary. 'What nonsense is this?' he asked, wondering how the information had got out. 'What do you know of my bone?'

'We know it fills your pots; that you alone have food while others go without and we come to beg the loan of this wonderful bone, so that the Monkeys' wedding feast may be a splendid one, a feast to be proud of, instead of a sorry affair that would disgrace us all.'

'No. I will not lend my bone!' The Lion growled and switched his tail angrily to and fro. 'Why should I lend my bone?' he muttered. 'I cannot spare it.' Then he had an inspiration. 'It would not work for Monkeys,' he said arrogantly.

'Indeed?' Kalulu raised an eyebrow. 'How can you tell? At least you can let the Monkeys try it. You cannot be so mean, so unkind as to refuse to help them. Remember, it is a wedding feast!'

Mkango shuffled his paws uncomfortably. He knew he ought to agree, but he didn't want the Monkeys to have his bone. He didn't want anyone to have it. He wanted to keep it to himself. But Kalulu was making it very difficult for him to give a flat refusal. He looked right and left and up at the sky, searching for some excuse. Not a cloud in sight, he noticed idly, not a sign of rain. Rain! . . . that was the answer! From the look of things, it would be weeks before the rains would break. He turned back to the deputation and there was a cunning smile on his face.

'Very well,' he said. 'The Monkeys may have my magic bone. . . .'

'Aah!' A long-drawn sigh of relief came from Kalulu and his friends.

'*As soon as it has rained.*' With an air of complete finality, Mkango, the Lion, stalked away in the direction of the river.

'But the wedding is in three days' time!' Kalulu called after him. 'We must have the bone now! Please let us have the bone.' Mkango took no notice.

'Oh, how unkind!' Kalulu looked at the Monkeys and the Monkeys looked at Kalulu. Nthanda's mouth was puckering as if she were going to cry.

'I thought it was g-going to be all right!' she wailed.

'There, there!' Kalulu took her hand and patted it comfortingly. 'It *is* going to be all right. All we have to do is to make it rain.'

The Monkeys gazed helplessly at the Rabbit. 'How can we do that?' they asked.

'Let me think.' Kalulu sat down, shut his eyes and laid his head on his paws. After a while he opened his eyes again, stroked one ear in a thoughtful sort of way and began to mutter to himself. Then he got up, walked over to the cave and examined the rocks, the ground and the great trees that grew all around, with the greatest care. 'Yes, plenty of cover,' he murmured. 'It is possible. It could be done!' Grinning from ear to ear, he went back to the Monkeys and explained his plan.

Every Monkey would be needed. Each one must bring a gourd. The gourds would be filled with water from the river and a chain of Monkeys would pass them along to those who would make the 'rain'. This would be done by more Monkeys, dozens of them, stationed in the trees above the cave. Each would hold a gourd that had been pierced with holes, into which the water would be poured. All must be done swiftly and silently.

'And we'll get Tandaubwe, the Spider, to hide in the cave and signal to us when the Lion wakes up. Then the rain must begin to fall.' Kalulu concluded his exposition and looked at Nyonyo and Nthanda for approval.

Their faces were alight with hope and admiration. 'It's a wonderful plan,' they cried happily. 'How clever you are, Kalulu! Let us go at once and call the Monkey troupes!'

Mkango, the Lion, had slept well and woke at midday, as was his habit. He yawned, stretched himself, decided he felt hungry and could do with a meal, so fetched his cooking pot. He peered into it and picked up the little white bone that lay all by itself at the bottom. He looked at it fondly. So those impudent Monkeys thought they were going to borrow it for their wretched wedding feast, did they? What impertinence! Well, he'd fobbed them off very cleverly. He had not refused to help them, oh, no! But he knew they would not dream of postponing the wedding and there certainly would be no rain within the next three days! With a very self-satisfied look on his face, Mkango dropped one bean into the cooking pot and placed the magic bone beside it, then walked to the mouth of the cave to have a look at the day.

The smile vanished fast enough when he saw the downpour. Goodness, how wrong he'd been! The heavy raindrops fell like a shower of diamonds on the parched earth; a steamy mist rose from the sun-scorched rocks and all but veiled the scene; little runnels of water made furrows in the dust. There was no doubt about it, the heavens had opened and the rain had come. With a feeling almost of awe, Mkango turned back into the cave. Could it be that Mlungu, the Great Spirit, was angry with him and had sent the rain as a sign of His displeasure? Perhaps he had been mean and foolish?

At all events, if the Monkeys still wanted it, he must now lend them his bone. Then, perhaps, Mlungu would forgive him and all would be well.

Comforted by this thought, the Lion returned to his cooking pot, which was now full of beans, but somehow he didn't feel hungry any more. Well, the beans would keep. He emptied the pot carefully into a shallow basket and again picked up the magic bone. It was still in his hand when he heard a discreet cough and looked up to see a very bedraggled Rabbit standing just inside the cave.

'Forgive me for entering so informally,' the Rabbit said courteously, 'but I thought you could not hear my shouts, the rain is beating down so hard. I have come for the magic bone you said you'd lend the Monkeys for their wedding feast.' Kalulu advanced into the cave and held out a dripping paw. 'So lucky that the rain has come in time,' he added, with a most disarming smile.

'It seems that Mlungu, the Great Spirit, wishes the Monkeys well and I can do no less.' Mkango spoke in sad and solemn tones. 'Here, take the bone and be sure to bring it back as soon as the feast is over.' He thrust the little white object into Kalulu's paw and, so chastened was his mood, that he even went so far as to escort the Rabbit back to the mouth of the cave. The rain was still pouring down and little pools of water were lying in the rocks.

'Well,' said Kalulu brightly, after expressing his thanks, 'you won't need to go to the river for a drink tonight! Plenty of water close at hand, is there not?'

The Lion nodded. That was some consolation, for he did not feel like seeing anyone in his present mood, not even the Rhinoceros.

The Rabbit left and, for a few minutes, Mkango stood and watched the rain. He thought it showed signs of lessening, but certainly it had been a heavy shower while it lasted. He felt thankful that there was no need for him to go out and get wet, like Kalulu. He hated getting wet. Perhaps, after all, he would have a meal and then go to sleep and try and forget how unwise he had been.

Meanwhile, Kalulu quickly let Nyonyo know that he had got the magic bone, then raced off with it to the Monkeys' *bwalo*, where Nthanda and the few elderly Monkeys who had not been making rain at once got busy with their cooking pots. Soon, with the aid of the bone, the pots were overflowing with beans and nuts and berries and, when one old grandmother produced a precious banana and it became a hundred and a hundred more, the Monkeys were overjoyed, for they knew that the success of their feast was now assured. Towards evening, the tired Monkey troupes came swinging home, but when they saw the mounds of food and brimming grain stores, they forgot their weariness and capered, laughed and chattered with delight. Now they could have a splendid feast! Now all was well and no one need be hungry any more. Now all their problems were solved!

Nadzikambe, the Chameleon, paused in his tale. The thought of all that food had made him feel quite hungry and he hurriedly swallowed two gnats whose insistent hum had been annoying him.

'Is that the end of the story?' asked Kamba, the Tortoise. 'Did the Lion never discover how he had been tricked?'

'Indeed he did,' replied the Chameleon. 'He found out on the evening of the wedding day. He had, as usual, gone down to the river for a drink—the puddles near his

cave had soon dried up—and he had met his friend, the Rhinoceros. The conversation turned, as it so often does, upon the weather. "That was a very heavy shower of rain we had the other day," Mkango had said.

'"What shower of rain?" queried the Rhinoceros. "What are you talking about? There's been no rain for months."

'"He means the Monkeys' rain," said someone, and several animals began to laugh. Then the story came out and Mkango realized that he had been fooled. He was furious, simply furious! In a terrible rage, he went bounding off to find the Monkeys' *bwalo*, but he was too late to spoil the wedding festivities. These had been concluded and the feast was almost at an end when the Monkeys heard the Lion's roaring. At once they took to the tree-tops and hid themselves away.'

'And what happened to the magic bone?' asked the Tortoise.

'Forgetting all about it in his fury, Mkango smashed every cooking pot that he could see and the fragments got scattered far and wide. And so the bone was lost.' The Chameleon shook his head. 'Some say it fell into an ant-heap, and that that is why there are so many ants. Some say that, when the rains came, it got washed into the river, and that that is why there are so many fish. Some say it must have reached the Great Water and come to rest beside a grain of salt, and that that is why the sea is so very salt. We shall never know the truth of the matter.'

'A pity,' sighed the Tortoise. 'One likes to know the truth!'

POSTSCRIPT
IF YOU ARE INTERESTED

THIS book has been written in response to a great many requests for 'One more book of the same kind, before you leave Africa!' So, the same kind it is, and I have still kept to the local names. These are Nyanja, except where two or more animals of the same kind appear in the same story. Then I have used the Tumbuka or Tonga equivalent. The next page will tell you how to pronounce them, if you do not already know. They are not really difficult once you get used to the general idea and can hum those 'Ms' and 'Ns'. If the tip of your tongue is pressed against your front teeth, you'll find it easy enough!

The proverbs come from various tribes, but they are mostly Nyanja, Tumbuka or Bemba.

ZOMBA,

NYASALAND

PRONUNCIATIONS

Achidu	Ah-chee-doo
Bambo	*Bah*-m'boh
Bangwe	*Bah*-n'gweh
Changa	*Chah*-n'gah
Chibethi	Chee-*beh*-tee
Chiuta	Chee-*oo*-tah
Chule	*Choo*-leh
Dziwa	*Dzee*-wah
Fisi	*Fee*-see
Garu	*Gah*-roo
Guapi	*Gwah*-pee
Herani	Heh-*rah*-nee
Kabawe	Kah-*bah*-weh
Kalulu	Kah-*loo*-loo
Kamba	*Kah*-m'bah
Kamodzi	Kah-*moh*-dzee
Kamwana	Kah-*mwah*-nah
Kanai	Kah-nye
Kasanu	Kah-*sah*-noo
Katatu	Kah-*tah*-too
Katumbu	Kah-*too*-m'boo
Kawiri	Kah-*wee*-ree
Khu-khu-khu	Koo-koo-koo
Khungubwe	Koo-n'*goo*-bweh
Mbalame	M'bah-*lah*-meh
Mbanda	M'*bah*-n'dah
Mbuzi	M'*boo*-zee
Mfuko	M'*foo*-koh
Mfumu	M'*foo*-moo
Mkango	M'*kah*-n'goh
Mkota	M'*koh*-tah
Mkuwi	M'*koo*-wee
Mlungu	M'*loo*-n'goo
Mpasa	M'*pah*-sah
Mphambe	M'*pah*-m'beh
Mpopo	M'*poh*-poh
Msoti	M'*soh*-tee
Msuku	M'*soo*-koo
Nadzikambe	Nah-dzee-*kah*-m'beh
Namazeze	Nah-mah-*zeh*-zeh
Ngamo	N-*gah*-moh
Ng'ona	N-*goh*-nah
Ngwina	N-*gwee*-nah
Njobvu	N-*joh*-b'voo
Nkhandwe	N-*kah*-n'dweh
Njusi	N-*joo*-see
Nkhope	N-*koh*-peh
Nkhuku	N-*koo*-koo
Nkhunda	N-*koo*-n'dah
Nthanda	N-*tah*-n'dah
Nthiwatiwa	N-*tee*-wah-tee-wah
Nungo	*Noo*-n'goh
Nyalugwe	Nee-yah-*loo*-gweh
Nyani	N'-*yah*-nee
Nyanja	N'*yah*-n'jah
Nyimbo	N'*yee*-m'boh
Nyole	N'*yoh*-leh
Nyonyo	N'*yoh*-n'yoh
Olé	Oh-leh
Sanjika	Sah-n'*jee*-kah
Tambala	Tah-m'*bah*-lah
Tandaubwe	Tah-n'dah-*oo*-bweh
Tikuona	Tee-koo-*oh*-nah
Ukaipa	Oo-kah-*ee*-pah
Vumbwe	*Voo*-m'bweh
Zikomo	Zee-*koh*-moh
Zonde	*Zoh*-n'deh